School Days

Pam Schiller

Special Needs Adaptations by Clarissa Willis

Acknowledgments

I would like to thank the following people for their contributions to this book. The special needs adaptations were written by Clarissa Willis. The CD is arranged by Patrick

Clarissa Willis   Patrick Brennan   Richele Bartkowiak

Brennan, and performed by Richele Bartkowiak and Patrick Brennan. It was engineered and mixed by Jeff Smith at Southwest Recordings. —Pam Schiller

Books written by Pam Schiller

The Bilingual Book of Rhymes, Songs, Stories, and Fingerplays, with Rafael Lara-Alecio and Beverly J. Irby

The Complete Book of Activities, Games, Stories, Props, Recipes, and Dances, with Jackie Silberg

The Complete Book of Rhymes, Songs, Poems, Fingerplays, and Chants, with Jackie Silberg

The Complete Daily Curriculum for Early Childhood: Over 1200 Easy Activities to Support Multiple Intelligences and Learning Styles, with Pat Phipps

The Complete Resource Book: An Early Childhood Curriculum, with Kay Hastings

The Complete Resource Book for Infants: Over 700 Experiences for Children From Birth to 18 Months

The Complete Resource Book for Toddlers and Twos: Over 2000 Experiences and Ideas

Count on Math: Activities for Small Hands and Lively Minds, with Lynne Peterson

Creating Readers: Over 1000 Games, Activities, Tongue Twisters, Fingerplays, Songs, and Stories to Get Children Excited About Reading

Do You Know the Muffin Man?, with Thomas Moore

The Instant Curriculum, Revised, with Joan Rosanno

The Practical Guide to Quality Child Care, with Patricia Carter Dyke

Start Smart: Building Brain Power in the Early Years

The Values Book, with Tamera Bryant

Where Is Thumbkin?, with Thomas Moore

School Days

CD INSIDE!

28 Songs and Over 300 Activities for Young Children

Pam Schiller

Gryphon House, Inc.
Beltsville, Maryland

Pam Schiller

School Days

© 2006 Pam Schiller
Printed in the United States of America.

Illustrations: Deborah Johnson
Cover Art: © 2002 Getty Images, Inc. gettyimages.com

Published by Gryphon House, Inc.
10726 Tucker Street, Beltsville, MD 20705
301.595.9500; 301.595.0051 (fax); 800.638.0928 (toll-free)

Visit us on the web at www.ghbooks.com

Library of Congress Cataloging-in-Publication Data

Schiller, Pamela Byrne.
   School days / Pam Schiller and Richele Bartkowiak ; illustrations, Deborah Johnson.
      p. cm.
   Includes bibliographical references and index.
   ISBN-13: 978-0-87659-019-5
   ISBN-10: 0-87659-019-9
   1. Language arts (Early childhood)--Activity programs. 2. Children's songs. 3. Early childhood education--Activity programs. I. Bartkowiak, Richele. II. Johnson, Deborah, ill. III. Title.
   LB1139.5.L35S354 2006
   372.21--dc22
                                        2006003274

Table of Contents

Introduction 7
Music in the Early Years 7
Thematic Content 7
Literacy Concepts 7
Optimizing Memory and Learning .8
Expanding Children's Learning With Activities 9
Modifications 9
    Special Needs 9
    English Language Learners 11
Involving English Language Learners in Music Activities 11
How to Use This Book 13
Bibliography 13

Songs and Activities 15
This Old Man 16
Sing a Song of Opposites 19
Days of the Week 22
The Alphabet Song 25
Good Morning to You 28
Nursery Rhyme Rap 31
Months of the Year 34
Great Green Gobs 37
Three Straight Sides 40
Clean Up 43
School Days 46
Miss Mary Mack 49
What Goes Together? 52
Can You Put the Toys Away? 55
Are You Listening? 57
Do You Know the Principal? 61
Grand Old Duke of York 64
MacNamara's Band 67
Johnny Works With One Hammer 70
Old MacDonald Has a Band 72
The Color Song 75
My Hands on My Head 79
I Like School 82
B-B-B Bubbles 85
Stop, Drop, and Roll 88
Rhyme Time 91

January

Bubbles in the Air 94
Happy Faces 97

More Learning and Fun 100
Songs 100
Poems and Chants 102
Fingerplays 103
Stories 103
Games 105
Recipes 106
Rebus Recipes 107
Sequence Cards 114
American Sign Language Signs 123
References and Bibliography 124

Indexes 124
Theme Index 124
Children's Book Index 124
Index 126

Introduction

Music in the Early Years

Music is a universal language, and singing is a hallmark of the early childhood classroom. Children love to sing! Teachers love to sing! Age makes no difference. Culture makes no difference.

Singing songs enriches thematic content, supports literacy concepts, and optimizes memory and learning. When you extend classroom activities, including modifications for special needs and English language learner populations, it is a perfect package. *School Days* is one of eight thematic book/CD sets that offer all of these resources in one package.

Thematic Content

School Days draws on several typical early childhood themes: Colors, Days of the Week, Numbers, Musical Instruments, Nursery Rhymes, Alphabet, and Safety. Read the lyrics and decide which songs best fit in your curriculum.

Each song is accompanied by a list of facts titled "Did You Know?" These facts provide background information about the song, interesting facts about the topic or lyrics, historical information, or some form of trivia you might use as a springboard to discussion. This will save you hours of research and add significantly to the value of the song.

Literacy Concepts

Young children need experiences that allow them to develop and practice basic literacy skills, such as listening, oral language development, phonological awareness, letter knowledge, print awareness, and comprehension. Suggestions for using the songs in *School Days* as a springboard for teaching these literacy skills accompany every title. Below is a definition of each literacy skill and the sub-skills they encompass.

○ **Listening:** the development of age-appropriate attention span, as well as the ability to listen for a variety of purposes; for example, details, directions, and sounds.

○ **Oral Language Development:** the acquisition of vocabulary, the fine-tuning of grammar, and the increase in sentence length and complexity.

○ **Phonological Awareness:** sensitivity to the sounds of language. Phonological awareness begins with babbling and cooing and goes all the way through the understanding of sound and symbol relationships and decoding. The skills in the higher end of the phonological awareness continuum--sound and symbol relationship and decoding--are appropriate for children who are age five or older.

○ **Segmentation:** the breaking apart of words by syllable or letter; for example, children clap the breaks in the word *di-no-saur*.

○ **Rhyme:** words that sound alike. The ending sound of the words is the same, but the initial consonant sound is different, for example, *cat* and *hat* or *rake* and *cake*.

○ **Alliteration:** the repetition of a consonant sound in a series of words; for example, *Peter Piper picked a peck of pickled peppers*. Children need to be able to hear the repetition of the /p/ sound, but do not need to identify that the sound is made by the letter "p".

○ **Onomatopoeia:** words that sound suggest the sound they are describing; for example, *pitter-patter, moo, quack, beep,* and so on.

○ **Letter Knowledge:** the visual recognition of each letter of the alphabet, both lowercase and uppercase.

○ **Print Awareness:** the understanding that print has many functions; for example, telling a story, making a list, as part of signs, in news articles, in recipes, and so on. It is also the awareness that print moves left to right and top to bottom.

○ **Comprehension:** the internalization of a story or a concept.

Optimizing Memory and Learning

Singing boosts memory and keeps the brain alert. Increased memory and alertness optimize the potential for learning. When we sing we generally feel good. That sense of well-being causes the brain to release endorphins into the blood stream and those endorphins act as a memory fixative. When we sing we automatically increase our oxygen intake, which, in turn, increases our alertness. Scientific research has validated what early childhood professionals know intuitively--that singing has a positive effect on learning.

Expanding Children's Learning With Activities

Using songs as a springboard for activities is a good way to bring the lyrics of the song into a meaningful context for children. Blowing bubbles after singing "Bubbles in the Air" reinforces and creates meaningful context for the specific characteristics of bubbles. Mixing bubble solution, drinking a bubbly drink, carrying a bubble across the playground, observing the colors of bubbles, and making bubble art prints after singing "B-B-B-Bubbles" helps children better understand the characteristics of bubbles, as well as the ways to use bubbles creatively for art and games.

Reading a book about bubbles after singing about bubbles also helps expand children's understanding. Literature selections are provided for each song. Integrating the teaching of themes and skills with songs, literature, and multidisciplinary activities provides a comprehensive approach for helping children recognize the patterns and the interconnected relationships of what they are learning.

Throughout the book, questions to ask children appear in italics. These questions are intended to help children think and reflect on what they have learned. This reflective process optimizes the opportunity for children to apply the information and experiences they have encountered.

Modifications

Suggestions for children with special needs and suggestions for English language learners accompany the song activities when appropriate. These features allow teachers to use the activities with diverse populations. All children love to sing and the benefits apply to all!

Special Needs

The inclusion of children with disabilities in preschool and child care programs is increasingly common. Parents, teachers, and researchers have found that children benefit in many ways from integrated programs that are designed to meet the needs of all children. Many children with disabilities, however, need accommodations to participate successfully in the general classroom.

Included in the extensions and activities for each song are adaptations for children with special needs. These adaptations allow all children to experience the song and related activities in a way that will maximize their learning opportunities. The adaptations are specifically for children who have needs in the following areas:

- ○ sensory integration
- ○ distractibility
- ○ hearing loss
- ○ spatial organization
- ○ language, receptive and expressive
- ○ fine motor coordination
- ○ cognitive challenges

The following general strategies from Kathleen Bulloch (2003) are for children who have difficulty listening and speaking.

Difficulty	Adaptations/Modifications/Strategies
Listening	○ State the objective--provide a reason for listening ○ Use a photo card ○ Give explanations in small, discrete steps ○ Be concise with verbal information: "Evan, please sit," instead of "Evan, would you please sit down in your chair?" ○ Provide visuals ○ Have the child repeat directions ○ Have the child close his eyes and try to visualize the information ○ Provide manipulative tasks ○ When giving directions to the class, leave a pause between each step so the child can carry out the process in her mind ○ Shorten the listening time required ○ Pre-teach difficult vocabulary and concepts
Verbal Expression	○ Provide a prompt, such as beginning the sentence for the child or giving a picture cue ○ Accept an alternate form of information-sharing, such as artistic creation, photos, charade or pantomime, and demonstration ○ Ask questions that require short answers ○ Specifically teaching body and language expression ○ First ask questions at the information level--giving facts and asking for facts back ○ Wait for children to respond; don't call on the first child to raise his hand ○ Have the child break in gradually by speaking in smaller groups and then in larger groups

English Language Learners

Strategies for English language learners are also provided to maximize the learning potential for English language learners.

The following are general strategies for working with English language learners (Gray, Fleischman, 2004-05):

○ **Keep the language simple.** Speak simply and clearly. Use short, complete sentences in a normal tone of voice. Avoid using slang, idioms, or figures of speech.

○ **Use actions and illustrations to reinforce oral statements.** Appropriate prompts and facial expressions help convey meaning.

○ **Ask for completion, not generation.** Ask children to choose answers from a list or to complete a partially finished sentence. Encourage children to use language as much as possible to gain confidence over time.

○ **Model correct usage and judiciously correct errors.** Use corrections to positively reinforce children's use of English. When English language learners make a mistake or use awkward language, they are often attempting to apply what they know about their first language to English. For example, a Spanish-speaking child may say, "It fell from me," a direct translation from Spanish, instead of "I dropped it."

○ **Use visual aids.** Present classroom content and information in a way that engages children--by using graphic organizers (word web, story maps, KWL charts), photographs, concrete materials, and graphs, for example.

Involving English Language Learners in Music Activities

Music is a universal language that draws people together. For English language learners, music can be a powerful vehicle for language learning and community-building. Music and singing are important to second language learners for many reasons, including:

○ The rhythms of music help children hear the sounds and intonation patterns of a new language.

○ Musical lyrics and accompanying motions help children learn new vocabulary.

○ Repetitive patterns of language in songs help children internalize the sentence structure of English.

○ Important cultural information is conveyed to young children in the themes of songs.

Strategies for involving English language learners in music activities vary according to the children's level of proficiency in the English language.

Level of Proficiency	Strategies
Beginning English Language Learners	o Keep the child near you and model motions as you engage in group singing. o Use hand gestures, movements, and signs as often as possible to accompany song lyrics, making sure to tie a specific motion to a specific word. o Refer to real objects in the environment that are named in a song. o Stress the intonation, sounds, and patterns in language by speaking the lyrics of the song while performing actions or referring to objects in the environment. o Use simple, more common vocabulary. For example, use round instead of circular.
Intermediate-Level English Language Learners	o Say the song before singing it, so children can hear the words and rhythms of the lyrics. o Use motions, gestures, and signs to help children internalize the meaning of song lyrics. Be sure the motion is tied clearly to the associated word. o Throughout the day, repeat the language patterns found in songs in various activities. o Stress the language patterns in songs, and pause as children fill in the blanks. o Adapt the patterns of song, using familiar vocabulary.
Advanced English Language Learners unfamiliar information.	o Use visuals to cue parts of a song. o Use graphic organizers to introduce o Use synonyms for words heard in songs to expand children's vocabulary. o Develop vocabulary through description and comparison. For example, it is round like a circle. It is circular. o Encourage children to make up new lyrics for songs.

How to Use This Book

Use the twenty-six songs on the *School Days* CD included with this book and the related activities in this book to enhance themes in your curriculum, or use them independently. Either way you have a rich treasure chest of creative ideas for your classroom.

The eight-package collection provides more than 200 songs, a perfect combination of the traditional best-loved children's songs and brand new selections created for each theme. Keep a song in your heart and put joy in your teaching!

Bibliography

Bulloch, K. 2003. *The mystery of modifying: Creative solutions.* Huntsville, TX: Education Service Center, Region VI.

Cavallaro, C. & M. Haney. 1999. *Preschool inclusion.* Baltimore, MD: Paul H. Brookes Publishing Company.

Gray, T. and S. Fleischman. Dec. 2004-Jan. 2005. "Research matters: Successful strategies for English language learners." *Educational Leadership,* 62, 84-85.

Hanniford, C. 1995. *Smart moves: Why learning is not all in your head.* Arlington, VA: Great Ocean Publications, p. 146.

LeDoux, J. 1993. "Emotional memory systems in the brain." *Behavioral and Brain Research,* 58.

Tabors, P. 1997. *One child, two languages: Children learning English as a second language.* Baltimore, MD: Paul H. Brookes Publishing Company.

Songs and Activities

This Old Man

This old man, he played one.
He played knick-knack on my thumb.
With a knick-knack paddy-whack,
Give a dog a bone.
This old man came rolling home.

This old man, he played two.
He played knick-knack on my shoe.
With a knick-knack paddy-whack,
Give a dog a bone.
This old man came rolling home.

Additional verses:
…three…on my knee…
…four…on the door…
…five…on a hive…
…six…sticks…
…seven…heaven…
…eight…gate…
…nine…line…
…ten…over again!

Vocabulary

again	man
bone	nine
dog	old
door	one
five	seven
four	shoe
eight	six
gate	sticks
heaven	ten
hive	thumb
home	three
knee	two
line	

Theme Connections

Animals
Counting
Numbers
Sounds

Did You Know?
○ "This Old Man" originated in England and is a favorite from British folklore. It has been recorded in many languages and is a popular children's song in most cultures.
○ "This Old Man" was sung by Bob Dylan on a Disney album in 1992.

Literacy Links

Oral Language
○ Ask a volunteer to show you how to play "knick-knack." Ask the children to say what they think "knick-knack" means.

Phonological Awareness

○ Challenge the children to think of additional words that rhyme with each number mentioned in the song.

○ Create a "Knick-Knack Paddy-Whack" movement pattern to accompany the words. For example, have the children chant "knick-knack paddy-whack" while slapping their knees twice, clapping twice, pulling first their left ear, then their right ear, and clapping twice. Continue chanting and moving to the chant. Now you know how to play the Knick-Knack Paddy-Whack game.

 English Language Learner Strategy: Help children understand that "rolling home" is just an imaginative way of saying, "walking home." Explain that "knick-knack" and "paddy-whack" are nonsense words.

Print Awareness

○ Photocopy, color, cut out, and laminate the This Old Man Rhyming Word Cards (pages 121-122). Display the cards as you sing the song.

○ Print numerals and number words on chart paper. Explain to the children that numbers can be represented by symbols (numerals) and also in words.

Special Needs Adaptation: For children with cognitive challenges, ask them to help you by holding up the number cards as you sing the song. If he does not know which card to hold up, point to the card you want him to hold up for all the children to see. Use this song as an opportunity to reinforce number concepts. Point out that this song involves numbers. Find objects around the room to count and look for numbers in everyday routines, such as two napkins, three blocks, two shoes, and so on.

Segmentation

○ Clap the syllables "knick-knack pad-dy-whack." *Are there more syllables than words? Which word has more than one syllable?*

Curriculum Connections

Fine Motor

○ Provide playdough and "paddy whackers" (tongue depressors). Invite the children to make playdough balls and then use their "paddy whackers" to flatten the dough.

○ Provide tempera paint and paper. Encourage the children to make thumbprints on the paper ("He played knick-knack on my thumb...").

Book Corner

This Old Man by
Pam Adams
This Old Man by
Carol Jones
*This Old Man: A Pop-
Up Song Book* by
Dick Dudley

Gross Motor

❍ Place two eight-foot strips of masking tape about four feet apart on the floor to create a road. Make a sign that says "home" and place it at one end of the masking tape strips. Challenge children to roll along the masking tape road to reach home. *Why is this hard to do?*

❍ Place a nine foot line of masking tape on the floor. Have the children walk the line, counting the steps it takes them to get to the end of the line. *Does it take less big steps than small steps to get to the end of the line?*

Language/Math

❍ Photocopy, color, cut out, and laminate the This Old Man Rhyming Word Cards (pages 121-122). Invite the children to match the numerals to the correct rhyming word. Encourage the children to sequence the numbers.

Math

❍ Provide six sticks of different lengths. Have the children arrange the sticks from the longest to the shortest and then rearrange them from shortest to longest. Have them arrange the sticks vertically and horizontally.

Music and Movement

❍ Offer the children rhythm band instruments to play while they sing the song.

Writing

❍ Print *knick-knack paddy-whack* on chart paper. Encourage the children to use markers to copy the words.

Home Connection

❍ Encourage the children to teach their families how to play Knick-Knack Paddy-Whack (see the second bullet under Phonological Awareness on the previous page).

Sing a Song of Opposites by Pam Schiller

Vocabulary

big
down
happy
opposites
sad
short
sing along
small
tall
up

(Tune: London Bridge Is Falling Down)
This is big and this is small.
This is big; this is small.
This is big and this is small.
Sing along with me.

Additional verses:
This is tall and this is short.
This is up and this is down.
This is sad and this is happy.

Big

Small

Theme Connections

Opposites
Under Construction

Did You Know?

○ Many educators believe that we learn best by exploring opposites. For example, we understand hot more completely when we experience cold. We understand dry by experiencing wet.

○ The first educator to write curriculum around the concept of opposites was the German educationalist, Friedrich Froebel.

Literacy Links

Comprehension
○ Teach the children the action story "Mrs. Wiggle and Mrs. Waggle" (pages 103-104).

Listening
○ Give each child a beanbag. Direct them to place the beanbag *over their head/under their foot*, *to their left/to their right*, and *in front of them/behind them*.

Oral Language

○ Fill a basket with pairs of opposites. Discuss the items with the children. Invite the children to create a new verse for the song.

 English Language Learner Strategy: Invite the children to use gestures instead of words to create pairs of opposites.

○ Discuss less tangible opposites such as day and night, happy and sad, and work and play.

○ Teach the children "Big and Small."

> **Big and Small**
> *I can make myself real big* (stand up on toes)
> *By standing up straight and tall*
> *But when I'm tired of being big,*
> *I can make myself get small.* (stoop down)

Print Awareness

○ Print the first verse of the song on sentence strips, leaving a blank space for the opposite words. Place the strips in a pocket chart. Print the opposite pairs in all the verses on sentence strips and cut the strips to the size of the word. Sing the song moving your hand under the words as you sing. Change the opposite pairs for each verse by sliding the opposites into the sentence strip.

Curriculum Connections

Art

○ Provide tempera paint, paper, and wide and narrow paintbrushes. Invite the children to paint wide and narrow lines on their paper.

Blocks

○ Encourage the children to build tall and short towers.

Discovery

○ Provide a basket of items that are soft (cotton balls and feathers), hard (washers and buttons), long (long ribbons and yarn), and short (short pieces of yarn or ribbon). Challenge the children to sort the items into opposite categories. *Do some items fit into more than one category?*

Exactly the Opposite
by Tana Hoban
Sing a Song of
Opposites by
Pam Schiller
Touch and Feel:
Opposites:
Garden by Ant
Parker

Fine Motor

○ Provide playdough. Invite the children to roll large and small balls and to make long and short snakes.

Language

○ Photocopy, color, cut out, and laminate the Opposite Cards (page 117). Challenge the children to find the opposite pairs.

> **Special Needs Adaptation:** Some children with special needs, especially those with autism spectrum disorder or a child with cognitive challenges, will have difficulty with less tangible opposite pairs. It will be easier for these children to understand the concept of opposite, if you use concrete objects or if you demonstrate opposite pairs for them. For example, turn the light off and say, "Off." Then, turn the light on and say, "On."

Music and Movement

○ Provide streamers and invite the children to dance to music with a slow tempo and music with a fast tempo.

Snack

○ Provide quiet snacks, such as bananas, yogurt, and gelatin, and noisy snacks, such as carrots, apples, and pretzels. Encourage the children to sort their snacks before they eat.

Story Time

○ Read a big book and a small book to the children.

Water Play

○ Place ice cubes, cups, and funnels in the water table. Invite the children to explore the opposites of slow and fast, warm and cold, full and empty, and sink and float as they play. Discuss the opposites as the children pour water and place items into the water.

Home Connection

○ Ask children to bring a pair of opposite items from home; for example, a soft candy and a hard candy or a big spoon and a little spoon. Allow children to present their opposite pairs during circle time or on a display table.

> **English Language Learner Strategy:** Encourage the children to sing the song using their pair of opposites.

Days of the Week

(Tune: The Addams' Family)
Days of the week (snap twice),
Days of the week (snap twice),
Days of the week, days of the week,
Days of the week. (snap twice)

There's Sunday and there's Monday.
There's Tuesday and there's Wednesday.
There's Thursday and there's Friday,
And then there's Saturday.

Days of the week (snap twice),
Days of the week (snap twice),
Days of the week, days of the week,
Days of the week. (snap twice)
(Repeat)

✓ **Special Needs Adaptation:** Children with limited motor skills may not be able to snap their fingers when you sing the song. Invite them to clap or tap on a drum, while the rest of the class snaps.

Vocabulary

days of the week
Friday
Monday
Saturday
Sunday
Thursday
Tuesday
Wednesday

Theme Connection

Day and Night

Did You Know?
○ One week equals 168 hours, 10,080 minutes, 604,800 seconds (except at daylight savings time transitions or leap year).
○ In many countries, the days of the weeks are named after the planets and Roman gods. For example, Saturday is named after the planet Saturn, Sunday after the Sun, and Monday after the moon. For the four other days, however, the names of Anglo-Saxon or Nordic gods have replaced the Roman gods that gave name to the planets. Tuesday is named after Tiw, the Norse god of war. Wednesday is named after Woden, the head of the Norse gods. Thursday is named after Thor, the Norse god of thunder, and Friday is named after Freya, the Norse god of beauty.

Literacy Links

Oral Language

○ Discuss common adjectives used with certain days of the week, such as blue Monday and freaky Friday. Print *TGIF* and the slogan *Thank God It's Friday* on chart paper. Draw a line under the first letter of each word in the slogan and point out that the acronym TGIF comes from the first letters of each word in the slogan.

○ Teach the children "Monday's Child." Explain what each line means because many of the words may be unfamiliar to the children.

Monday's Child

Monday's child is fair of face,
Tuesday's child is full of grace,
Wednesday's child is full of woe,
Thursday's child has far to go,
Friday's child is loving and giving,
Saturday's child works hard for his living,
And the child that is born on the Sabbath day
Is bonny and blithe, and good and gay.

November						
Sun	Mon	Tue	Wed	Thu	Fri	Sat
	1	2	3	4	5	6
7	8	9	10	11	12	13
14	15	16	17	18	19	20
21	22	23	24	25	26	27
28	29	30				

Print Awareness

○ Show the children the days of the week on a calendar. Show the repetition of days each week.

○ Print the days of the week on chart paper. Point out that the last three letters in each word are the same (*day*). This is why all the days of the week end with the same sound.

Segmentation

○ Print the days of the week on chart paper. Have the children clap the syllables in each word. Print a numeral beside each name to indicate the number of syllables. *Which day of the week has the most syllables?*

Curriculum Connections

Fine Motor

○ Photocopy a calendar page. Cut the photocopy into separate squares for each day. Invite the children to match the cut squares to the original calendar page.

Book Corner

Alexander, Who Used to Be Rich Last Sunday by Judith Viorst

One Windy Wednesday by Phyllis Root

Today Is Monday by Eric Carle

Tuesday by David Wiesner

The Very Hungry Caterpillar by Eric Carle

Wacky Wednesday by Dr. Seuss (Theo LeSeig)

Gross Motor
○ Use masking tape to create a seven-box hopscotch grid on the floor. Have the children hop the grid while chanting the days of the week.

Language
○ Print each day of the week on a separate sentence strip of paper, leaving a space between the first part of each word and *day*. Laminate the sentence strips and make a puzzle cut between the first part of the word and *day*. Invite the children to work the puzzles to restore all the days of the weeks.
○ Cut ads from magazines and newspaper that have one or more days of the week mentioned in them. Laminate the ads and have the children search the ads for days of the week. Provide a crayon to use to circle the days that they find.

Math
○ Provide a variety of items, such as craft sticks, buttons, and washers. Have the children count seven of each item into a box.

Music
○ Sing "The Mulberry Bush" (page 100). Encourage the children to make up new verses to the song.

Story Time
○ Read *Wacky Wednesday* by Dr. Seuss (Theo LeSeig) to the children and then let them help you set up a Wacky Wednesday in the classroom. Turn tables upside down, place books or blocks in places they obviously do not belong, and other wacky arrangements.

Writing
○ Print the days of the week on chart paper. Invite the children to copy the days of the weeks using magnetic letters.

Home Connection

○ Encourage the children to find out which day of the week they were born on. When the children return to school, graph the results of their research. On which were the most children born? The least?

The Alphabet Song

Vocabulary

ABCs
backwards
expected
know
ZYXs

Theme Connections

Me
Opposites

A - B - C - D - E - F - G,
H - I - J - K - L - M - N - O - P, Q - R - S,
T - U - V,
W - X,
Y and Z.
Now I know my ABCs.
Next time sing them backwards with me.

Z - Y - X - W - V - U - T,
S - R - Q - P - O - N - M, L - K - J,
I - H - G,
F - E - D,
C - B - A.
Now I've said my ZYXs.
Bet that's not what you expected!

Did You Know?

○ The alphabet is used for writing and has, theoretically, a one-for-one relationship between a character (or letter) and a phoneme (sound). Few alphabets, including the English alphabet, have achieved this ideal exactness.

○ Reciting the alphabet the same way every time, from A to Z, encourages children to memorize it and learn it by rote. When it is learned by rote, it is stored in the lowest functioning part of the brain, making it difficult to access in rational thought. By saying the alphabet forwards and backwards and even starting from the middle, children learn that the alphabet can be used in many combinations. It is not always arranged from A to Z. Children need to see that it can be organized by letters that have all straight lines, letters that have only curved lines, and so on. This helps them see the fluidity of the letters, which causes the knowledge of letters to be stored in rational thought. When children are exposed to many different way of organizing letter, the brain stores the information in rational thought—the highest functioning part of the brain. This allows the child to have access to the information in ways that encourage him or her to use the information divergently. When children learn information by rote—always the same pattern—the information gets stored in a lower-functioning part of the brain.

Literacy Links

Letter Knowledge
○ Write the alphabet on chart paper. Ask the children to help you identify the letters that are written with all straight lines (such as A and E).
○ Ask each child to point to or name the letter of the alphabet that is the first one in his or her name.

Listening
○ Sing the song. Have each child stand up when the group sings the first letter of his or her name.

Phonological Awareness
○ Select a letter, for example, "J". Have each child say his or her name, changing the beginning sound to the sound of the selected letter. For example, Sam will pronounce his name *Jam,* Mandy will pronounce her name *Jandy,* and so on.

Curriculum Connections

Dramatic Play
○ Provide magnetic or felt letters and invite the children to make and serve "alphabet soup."

Fine Motor
○ Provide playdough and have the children shape the first letter of their names.

Games
○ Have an Alphabet Hunt. Hide alphabet cards around the room. Invite the children to find the cards. After all the letters are found, have the children place them on the floor from Z to A.

Language
○ Provide magnetic letters and ask the children to line the letters up from A to Z and then from Z to A.
○ Provide children with a set of alphabet cards. Have them sort the letters into letters with straight lines (F), letters with curves (C), and letters with both straight lines and curved lines (P).

Movement

❍ Have the children work in pairs. Call out a letter of the alphabet and ask them to make the letter using their bodies. Continue until you finish the alphabet or children tire of the game.

Snack

❍ Provide the Letter Pretzel Rebus Recipe (page 113). Have each child make a letter pretzel that represents the first letter of his or her name.

Writing

❍ Provide cereal-shaped letters and encourage the children to use the letters to spell their names. When they are finished, they can eat their "names."

Alphabet Adventure by Audrey and Bruce Wood
Alphabet Mystery by Audrey and Bruce Wood
Chicka Chicka Boom Boom by Bill Martin, Jr. and John Archambault
Eating the Alphabet by Lois Ehlert

Home Connection

❍ Ask the children to make a list of the first letter in the first name of each of their family members. Have the children bring their list back to school. Graph the results. *Which letter is used the most? Which letter is used the least?*

Good Morning to You

with additional verses by Pam Schiller

Good morning to you!
Good morning to you!
We're all in our places
With bright, shining faces.
This is the way to start a great day!

Good afternoon to you!
Good afternoon to you!
We're all in our places
With food on our faces.
This is the way to have a great day!

Good evening to you!
Good evening to you!
Stars and moon in their places,
As they go through their paces.
This is the way to end a great day!

Vocabulary

day
end
faces
food
good morning
great
moon
paces
places
stars
start

Theme Connections

Family
Friends

Did You Know?

❍ "Good morning" is a familiar greeting in many countries. For information on how to say "Good morning" in 165 language, visit http://www.elite.net/~runner/jennifers/gmorning.htm.

❍ Many versions of this song are used in early childhood classrooms as a morning circle song (page 100).

Literacy Links

Comprehension

❍ Print *goodnight* on a sheet of chart paper. Draw a line between *good* and *night*. Point out that goodnight is two words that join together to make up one word, which is called a *compound word*.

○ Teach the children to say "hello" in other languages. Teach them to say *hello* using America Sign Language (page 123).

Cantonese	Néih hóu
Cherokee	O-si-yo
Creole	Bon jou
Danish	God dag
Dutch	Hallo
Finnish	Päivää
French	Bonjour
German	Guten Tag
Hebrew [formal]	Shalom
Italian	Buon giorno
Japanese	Konnichi wa
Navajo	Yá'át'ééh
Spanish	Hola

Oral Language

○ Practice greetings and responses. For example, if someone says, "Hello" you say, "Hello." If someone says, "Good morning" you respond with "Good morning." If someone says, "How are you?" you say, "Well, thank you." Sing "Where Is Thumbkin?" (page 103).

Curriculum Connections

Art

○ Provide white or light blue construction paper and crayons. Invite the children to draw a daytime picture. Provide black or dark blue construction paper and white chalk. Invite the children to draw a nighttime picture.

Construction/Language

○ Give each child an eight-inch paper plate. Have them draw a sunny, wakeful face on one side and a sleeping face on the other side. Provide a tongue depressor so that the children can make their faces into puppet. Encourage them to interact with one another using their plates to inspire dialogue.

Book Corner

Good Morning, Good Night by Teresa Imperato

Good Morning, Sam by Marie-Louise Gay

Good Night, Sam by Marie-Louise Gay

Goodnight Max by Rosemary Wells

Goodnight Moon by Margaret Wise Brown

Hello! Good-Bye! by Aliki

The Napping House by Audrey Wood

Language

○ Photocopy, color, and laminate the Day and Night Sorting Cards (page 116). Invite the children to sort the cards into daytime and nighttime activities.

○ Photocopy, color, cut out, and laminate the Brushing My Teeth Sequence Cards (page 114). Invite the children to sequence the cards. Teach them the song, "This Is the Way We Brush Our Teeth" (page 102).

Math

○ `Give the children ten large wiggle eyes and a paper cup. The children put the eyes in the cup, shake them, and then dump them on a tray. Ask the children to sort the eyes into those that land face up (wakeful eyes) and those that land face down (sleeping eyes) to determine if there are more wakeful or more sleeping eyes.

Music

○ Sing alternative versions (version 2 and 3) of "Good Morning to You" (page 100).

Sand Table Play

○ Dump confetti stars into the sand table. Provide strainers and invite the children to search for the stars.

Writing

○ Print *Good Morning* and *Goodnight* on chart paper. Provide magnetic letters and encourage the children to copy the greetings.

Home Connection

○ Encourage the children to teach their family members how to say "hello" in one of the languages they learned.

Nursery Rhyme Rap

Vocabulary

barn   meadow
blow   moon
clock   mouse
cow   one
crown   over
curds and whey
dish   pail
down   sheep
fall   sight
fast asleep   spider
fiddle   spoon
frightened   struck
haystack   tuffet
hill   tumbling
horn   under
jumped   wall
king's horses
king's men

Theme Connections

Humor
Nursery Rhymes

(Tune: Ninety Nine Bottle of Pop on the Wall)
Jack and Jill went up the hill,
To get a pail of water.
Jack fell down and broke his crown,
And Jill came tumbling after.

Chorus:
Oh, A B C D E F G...H I J K L...
M N O P...Q R S...T U V W X Y Z!

Humpty Dumpty sat on a wall.
Humpty Dumpty had a great fall.
All the king's horses and all the king's men,
Couldn't put Humpty together again.

(Chorus)

Little Miss Muffet sat on a tuffet,
Eating her curds and whey.
Along came a spider and sat down beside her,
And frightened Miss Muffet away!

(Chorus)

Hey, diddle diddle, the cat and the fiddle,
The cow jumped over the moon.
The little dog laughed to see such sport,
And the dish ran away with the spoon!

(Chorus)

Little Boy Blue, come blow your horn.
The sheep's in the meadow,
The cow's in the corn.
Where is the boy who looks after the sheep?
He's under the haystack fast asleep!

(Chorus)

Hickory dickory dock!
The mouse ran up the clock!
The clock struck one, the mouse ran down!
Hickory dickory dock!

(Chorus)

Did You Know?

❍ Many nursery rhymes reflect events in history. Two examples are "Ring Around the Rosie," which refers to the Bubonic plague and "Remember, Remember," which alludes to Guy Fawkes' foiled attempt to blow up the English Houses of Parliament! Because direct dissent might be punishable by death, people used nursery rhyme lyrics to parody the royal and political events of the day.

❍ Little Miss Muffet was a young girl named Patience Muffet. Her stepfather, Dr. Muffet (1553-1604) was a famous entomologist who wrote the first scientific catalogue of British insects. While eating her breakfast of curds and whey, Little Miss Muffet was frightened by one of his spiders and ran away!

Literacy Links

Letter Knowledge

❍ Print *Hey Diddle Diddle* on chart paper. Ask the children to identify the letters in the words. *Which letter appears the most?*

Phonological Awareness

❍ Recite two or three of the nursery rhymes in a whisper until you get to the rhyming word. Say those words in a normal voice.

❍ Recite the rhymes, stopping on rhyming words and having the children fill them in.

❍ Print *Hey Diddle Diddle* on chart paper. Point out the repetition of the /d/ sound in Diddle Diddle. Tell the children that when a beginning consonant sound is repeated in a series of words it is called *alliteration*. *Can anyone think of another rhyme with alliteration?* (Little Boy Blue)

Curriculum Connections

Art

❍ Provide fingerpaint, drawing paper, and markers. Encourage the children to make fingerprint mice by adding mouse features (ears, whiskers, and tails) to fingerprints.

Blocks

❍ Provide farm props and plastic farm animals for dramatic play. Have the children use shredded paper to build a haystack for Little Boy Blue.

Construction

○ Provide four black pipe cleaners. Show the children how to twist the pipe cleaners in the middle to make a spider with eight legs. Help the children shape the legs and then tie piece of elastic string or a rubble band to the center of the spider so that children can make it dance by jiggling the string.

Discovery/Blocks

○ Provide blocks and plastic eggs. Invite the children to build a wall for Humpty Dumpty. Challenge them to balance the eggs on their wall.

Dramatic Play

○ Provide a light source. Show the children how to wiggle their finger between the light source and the wall to create shadow spiders on the wall.

○ Crumple newspaper to make a hill. Cover the hill with a sheet or piece of fabric. Decorate two empty toilet paper tubes to look like a Jack and a Jill. Draw faces on one end of each tube and glue on yarn hair. Invite the children to make Jack and Jill go up and down the hill.

Fine Motor

○ Cut oval (egg) shapes from construction paper. Draw a face on the eggs to create Humpty Dumptys. Laminate the Humpty Dumptys and cut them into puzzle pieces. Have the children put a Humpty Dumpty puzzle together.

Gross Motor

○ Use masking tape to outline a moon shape on the floor. Invite the children to jump over the moon.

Snack

○ Serve curds and whey (cottage cheese) for snack. Add a little fruit to help entice children to eat it.

Home Connection

○ Suggest that the children teach their family one of the nursery rhymes.

Book Corner

Animal Crackers: A Delectable Collection of Pictures, Poems, and Lullabies for the Very Young by Jane Dyer

The Real Mother Goose by Blanche Fisher Wright

The Real Mother Goose Color Rhymes by Josie Yee

The Real Mother Goose Sing-Along Rhymes by Josie Yee

SONGS AND ACTIVITIES

Months of the Year

(Tune: Bumpin' Up and Down in My Little Red Wagon)
January, February, March, and April,
May, June, July, and August,
September, October, November, December,
Let's start all over again.

January, February, March, and April
May, June, July and August,
September, October, November, December,
Twelve months in a year.

Vocabulary

April
August
December
February
January
July
June
March
May
months
months of the year
November
October
September
twelve
year

Theme Connections

Seasons

Did You Know?

❍ A calendar is used to look at time in the past or future, to show how many days until a certain event takes place, or to figure out how long since something important happened.

❍ Although we celebrate our birthday every year, our actual birthday only occurs once every seven years! Not counting leap years, the date we were born on moves each year to the following day of the week. For example, if you were born on Saturday March 15th, in the following year March 15th will fall on a Sunday, the year after on a Monday, and so on. This means your annual celebration is actually for your birth date, not your birthday. In truth, your birth day (the actual day you were born) occurs only every seven years.

Literacy Links

Oral Language

❍ Teach the children the American Sign Language sign for *Happy Birthday* (page 123).

English Language Learner Strategy: It is not customary in every culture to celebrate a child's birthday on the anniversary of his or her birth. Birthdays are celebrated in different ways around the world. Check with families ahead of time to find out how the child's birthday is celebrated. Help all the children learn that there are many ways to celebrate a birthday.

○ Ask the children what month they were born in. Help them learn to say their birth date.

○ Teach the children "Thirty Days."

Thirty Days

Thirty days hath September,
April, June, and November;
All the rest have thirty-one,
Excepting February alone,
And it has twenty-eight days time,
But in leap years, February has twenty-nine.

Print Awareness

○ Print the song on chart paper. Move your hand under the words as you sing. Point out the top-to-bottom and left-to-right progression of the words.

Curriculum Connections

Dramatic Play

○ Provide birthday props, including hats, plates, and cups. Encourage the children to pretend to have a birthday party.

Gross Motor

○ Create a 12-space hopscotch grid on the floor with masking tape. Have the children recite the months of the year as they hop through the grid. Add a visual element to this activity by photocopying, coloring, cutting out, and laminating the Months of the Year Picture Cards (pages 118-119). Place the corresponding card in each square of the hopscotch grid.

Language

○ Photocopy, color, cut out, and laminate the Months of the Year Picture Cards (pages 118-119). Challenge children to arrange the cards in order from January to December.

Book Corner

Chicken Soup and Rice: A Book of Months by Maurice Sendak

Parade Day: Marching Through the Calendar by Bob Barner

Twelve Hats for Lena: A Book of Months by Karen Katz

Library

❍ Collect old calendars for the children to look at and compare.

Math

❍ Make a graph of the children's birthdays. *Are there more births in one month than in the other months?*

Music

❍ Sing songs and recite poems and fingerplays that have months mentioned in them "Miss Mary Mack" (page 49), "April Clouds" (page 103), "Five Little Snowmen" (page 103), and "In the Merry, Merry Month of May" (page 101).

Writing

❍ Print the months of the year on chart paper and encourage the children to use magnetic letters to copy them.

Home Connection

❍ Encourage the children to ask each of their family members in which month they were born. Graph the results of their research. Which month has the most birthdays?

Great Green Gobs

Vocabulary

frogs
gobs
grass
great
green
leaves
peas

Theme Connections

Colors
Food

by Pam Schiller

(Tune: Row, Row, Row Your Boat)
Great green gobs of grass.
Great green gobs of peas.
Grass and peas, peas and grass,
All in great green gobs.

Great green gobs of frogs.
Great green gobs of leaves.
Frogs and leaves, leaves and frogs,
All in great green gobs.

Did You Know?

○ Green is a common color in nature. Many plants have chlorophyll, which is a complex chemical that makes plants green.
○ In the Middle Ages, green represented evil or demonic beings (including dragons) and sometimes love.
○ Green symbolizes *go* because of how it is used in traffic signals. Along the highway, information and direction signs are often green.
○ Green is used in night-vision goggles because the human eye is most sensitive and able to discern the most shades in that color.
○ In auto racing, a green flag signals the start or resumption of a race.
○ Because of its ability to camouflage, green is typically used for the field uniforms for many military services. It is also used as the dress uniform for many land armies and marines.
○ Green is a symbol of Ireland, which is often referred to as "the Emerald Isle."

Literacy Links

Listening
○ Read the words to the song slowly. Have the children raise their hands each time they hear something mentioned in the song that is green.

Oral Language
❍ Discuss the use of green in phrases such as *green with envy*, *in the green*, and *green-eyed monster*.
❍ Teach the children the American Sign Language sign for *green* (page 123).

Oral Language/Print Awareness
❍ Talk about things that are green. Invite the children to brainstorm a list of green things. Write their list on chart paper.

Phonological Awareness
❍ Print *Great Green Gobs* on chart paper. Ask the children to identify the first letter of each word. Say the words slowly and ask the children to listen carefully for a repeated sound. Explain that a repetitive sound that occurs in a phrase or a sentence is called *alliteration*. Challenge the children to say "Great Green Gobs" three times quickly.

Curriculum Connections

Art
❍ Provide paper, paintbrushes, and a variety of shades of green tempera paint. Invite the children to paint a monochromatic green painting.

Dramatic Play
❍ Fill the center with green dress-up clothes. Invite the children to dress in green.

Fine Motor
❍ Mix Green Goop. Heat 2 cups salt and 1 cup water for 4 to 5 minutes. Remove from heat and add 1 cup cornstarch and ½ cup water. Stir until mixture thickens. Add a few drops of green food coloring. Store the Goop in re-sealable plastic bags.

Games
❍ Hide green construction paper circles in the classroom. Invite the children to find them.

Math
❍ Provide green (light and dark) construction paper shapes. Invite the children to create patterns (for example, light/light/dark, light/light/dark).

Book Corner

The Berenstain Bears and the Green-Eyed Monster by Stan and Jan Berenstain

Five Green and Speckled Frogs by Priscilla Burris

Go Away, Big Green Monster! by Ed Emberley

Green Eggs and Ham by Dr. Seuss

✓ **Special Needs Adaptation:** For children with visual or cognitive challenges, use thick paper or felt. Invite the child to take his finger and trace around the edge of each shape. Make sentences that help the child identify other objects in the room that are the same shape as his green one.

Outdoors

❍ Play Red Light, Green Light. Select a child to be IT. Have IT stand on one side of the playground and the other children in a line on the other side of the playground. Have IT turn her back to the group and say, "Green light." The children start to run toward IT. IT calls, "Red light" and turns around. Every child must stop running on the call of "red light." If IT catches a child still running, that child becomes the new IT. Continue the game until the children tire of it.

Science

❍ Provide photos of animals, including some that are green. Have the children sort the animals by those that are green and those that are not green.

Snack

❍ Invite the children to follow the Green Drink Rebus Recipe (page 110) to make their snack.

Home Connection

❍ Ask each child to bring in a green item from home. Place the green items on a display table for all to see.

Three Straight Sides

by Pam Schiller

(Tune: Three Blind Mice)
Three straight sides,
Three straight sides,
See how they meet.
See how they meet.
They follow the path that a triangle makes.
Just three sides and that's all it takes.
They make a triangle for heaven sakes.
Three straight sides,
Three straight sides,
Three…straight…sides!

Vocabulary

follow
heaven
meet
path
side
straight
three
triangle

Theme Connections

Counting
Shapes and Sizes

Did You Know?

○ A triangle is a shape formed by three straight lines meeting at three different points. The three intersection points are triangle vertices. The line segments between the vertices are triangle sides.
○ A triangle can also be defined as a three-sided polygon.
○ Triangles are classified according to the relative lengths of their sides:
  ○ All the sides of an *equilateral triangle* are equal in length, and all the angles are the same—60°.
  ○ An *isosceles triangle* has two sides equal in length, and two equal internal angles.
  ○ A *scalene triangle* has sides that are different lengths, and internal angles that are all different.

Literacy Links

Comprehension
○ Teach the children the American Sign Language sign for *triangle* (page 124).

O Put children into groups of three. Help them form three straight lines and then join together to make a human triangle.

Comprehension/Letter Knowledge

O Print *triangle* on chart paper. Have the children identify the first three letters, *tri*. Circle the first three letters and pronounce the word they make. Explain that *tri* means three and is used in words to mean the same thing. Examples include tricycle, triathlon, and triad. Print each example on chart paper and circle the first three letters.

Oral Language

O Talk about triangles. Show several examples of a triangle. Encourage children to name things that have a triangular shape.

Curriculum Connections

Art

O Cut easel paper into triangular shapes. Provide paint, and invite the children to paint on the triangles.
O Provide triangular templates, paper, and crayons and markers. Encourage the children to use the templates to create designs.
O Provide triangular-shaped sponges, paint, and paper. Invite the children to create a triangular painting.

Blocks

O Challenge children to build a structure using only triangular blocks.

Fine Motor

O Provide playdough. Encourage the children to roll playdough into three snake shapes and then connect the snakes to make a triangle.
O Provide pipe cleaners and encourage the children to connect three pipe cleaners to make a triangle.

Games

O Have the children sit in groups of three in a triangular position, with legs spread out straight and touching one foot to the foot of the child next to them. Give each group a beanbag and have the group of three toss the beanbag, counting to three as each person catches the beanbag.

Book Corner

The Greedy Triangle by Marilyn Burns
Shapes, Shapes, Shapes by Tana Hoban
Triangles by Sarah L. Schuette

Gross Motor

○ Use masking tape to make large triangles on the floor. Challenge the children to walk the triangles with a beanbag on their heads.

Math

○ Provide construction paper triangles in different sizes and colors. Invite the children to sort the triangles by color and/or size. Have them create patterns with the triangles.

Writing

○ Print *triangle*, *square*, and *circle* on chart paper. Draw the shape next to the word. Have the children use magnetic letters copy the words

Home Connection

○ Have the children bring a triangular shaped item to school. Invite the children to describe their item to the class.

Clean Up

Vocabulary

clean
clean up
everybody
everywhere
share

Clean up, clean up.
Everybody, everywhere.
Clean up, clean up.
Everybody do your share.
(Repeat)

Theme Connections

Family
Friends
Toys

Did You Know?

○ Keeping things clean in our surroundings helps us stay safe and healthy.

○ There are federal, regional, state, and local government agencies that have the job of helping to clean up things in the environment that are hazardous to our health. Since 1970, the amount of money spent has more than doubled. *(Statistical Abstract of the United States, 114th edition.* Issued by the U.S. Department of Commerce. U.S. Government Printing Office, Washington, D.C., 1994.)

○ A clean environment is an important global issue. In 1972, the United Nations Environment Programme (UNEP) was formed. It is a substantial organization engaged in information exchange and coordination of national programs for environmental protection. In 1991, UNEP and the World Bank, created a Global Environment Facility to serve as the principle multilateral mechanism to provide funds to developing countries for complying with environmental commitments.

○ See "Can You Put the Toys Away?" on page 55 for more information about toys and cleanup time.

Literacy Links

Oral Language

○ Talk about *messy* and *clean. What does the room look like when it is messy? Why is it a good idea to keep the room clean? What happens to toys when they are spread all over the floor? How can you find what you are looking for when it is not where it belongs?*

- Discuss the safety issues related to a clean room. For example, when toys are picked up, the likelihood of someone tripping is reduced. When spills are cleaned up, it prevents someone from slipping. When loose cords are put away, it reduces the danger of tripping over the cord.
- Talk about cleanup rules. Demonstrate putting things where they belong. How do children know where things go?
- Discuss sharing the workload. Ask children how they feel when they are left alone with a mess.

Curriculum Connections

Blocks
- Have the children sort the blocks according to their shapes. Explain that when putting the blocks away, they can organize them by shape (squares together, rectangles together, and so on).

Dramatic Play
- Provide cleaning items, such as brooms, mops, empty spray bottles, and sponges, and invite the children to pretend to clean a house.

Fine Motor
- Provide shredded paper and a small dustpan and hand broom. Have the children sweep the paper into the dustpan and discard it into a paper bag. If the children need (or want) more practice cleaning up the shredded paper, they can empty the bag and clean it up again.

Games
- Play cooperative games like Cooperative Musical Circles (page 105) or Tug of Peace (page 105).

Math
- Give the children washcloths or small towels to fold. Challenge them to fold the cloths into rectangles and squares.

Outdoors
- Take the classroom chairs outdoors. Provide soapy water and sponges. Invite the children to clean the chairs.
- Give children a paper bag and have them clean up the litter on the playground. (**Safety Note**: Be sure the children wear sturdy work clothes for protection. Remind children not to pick up broken pieces of glass or anything with a sharp edge.)

Book Corner

Max Cleans Up by Rosemary Wells

Newton and the Big Mess by Rory Tyger

Pigsty by Mark Teague

Who Made This Big Mess? by Andrew Gutelle

Snack

○ Make peanut butter and jelly sandwiches. Cut them in half. Have the children select a partner and share a sandwich. **Allergy Warning**: Check for allergies before serving peanut butter or any other food to children.

Social Studies

○ Make a helper chart. Use it to assign classroom tasks, such as line captain, door holder, and so on.

Water Play

○ In a dishpan or the sand and water table, provide a sponge, a dish cloth, and paper towels. *Which item soaks up water easiest? Which item would you use if you were cleaning up spilled milk?*

○ See page 56 in "Can You Put the Toys Away?" for additional activities for toys and cleanup time.

Home Connection

○ Suggest that the children help clean up after dinner tonight.

School Days

School days, school days,
Dear, old golden rule days
Reading and writing and 'rithmatic,
Taught by a teacher who's very strict.
You were my queen in calico.
I was your bashful, barefoot beau.
You wrote in ink, "I love you, Joe,"
When we were a couple of kids.

Vocabulary

arithmetic
barefoot
bashful
beau
calico
couple
dear
golden rule
ink
old
queen
reading
school
strict
teacher
writing

Theme Connections

Community Workers
Friends

Did You Know?

○ School has not always been a requirement. In 1900, many thirteen-year-olds went to work. Some worked at jobs adults couldn't do, such as crawling into small places to fix or change machinery parts—and many didn't survive. Others worked the same long shifts as their parents. Some sold newspapers, sewed clothing, or cleaned chimneys.

○ In the early 20th century, students attended public schools to learn so that they would find a job. All of the grades were taught in one room by one teacher. Depending on when students started school, they usually graduated about the time when children today might finish middle school. Then they had to find full-time jobs.

○ For more information about schools see School Days Facts (page 105) .

Literacy Links

Comprehension

○ Read "I Like School" (page 104) to the children. Create flannel board pieces for the story and ask the children to help you retell the story using the flannel board pieces. Ask questions. *Which activity in the story sounds like the most fun to you? How are the activities in the story like those we do in our classroom?*

Oral Language

○ Talk about the rules at school. Write the rules on chart paper and encourage the children to illustrate the list.

○ Teach the children the American Sign Language signs for *school* and *I love you* (page 123).

Print Awareness

○ Print the song on chart paper. Move your hand under the words as you sing them. Help the children see the top-to-bottom and left-to-right progression of the print.

Curriculum Connections

Art

○ Provide calico print fabric or wallpaper samples. Invite the children to make calico collages.

○ Provide a pan of tempera paint, paper, and a tub of soapy water. Invite the children to take off their shoes and socks, step in the paint, and then onto their paper to make "barefoot" footprints. **Note**: It may be slippery to walk on the paper. Hold each child's hand as he or she walks on the paper.

Dramatic Play

○ Provide props such as books, paper, book bags, lunch kits, pencils, and so on. Invite the children to play school.

Language

○ Invite the children to draw a picture of their favorite school activity and then dictate a sentence to you that describes the activity. Print their sentence at the bottom of the drawing or on the back of the drawing.

Book Corner

First Day Jitters by
   Julie Danneberg
First Day, Hooray! by
   Nancy Poydar
Hurray for Pre-K by
   Ellen B. Senisi
*Miss Bindergarten
   Gets Ready for
   Kindergarten* by
   Joseph Slate

Library

○ Provide books for the children to "read" to each other.

Math

○ Provide five lunch bags. Provide pretend lunch items to pack, such as plastic play foods. Have the children pack one item in each bag.

Music and Movement

○ Invite the children to dance creatively with scarves or streamers.

Writing

○ Give the children writing slates and chalk and encourage them to write their names on the slates. If slates are unavailable use drawing paper or chalk boards.

○ Print *I love you* on chart paper and invite the children to copy the phrase on slates or on drawing paper.

Home Connection

○ Encourage the children to talk with their families about their school experiences.

Miss Mary Mack

Vocabulary

black
buttons
down
dressed
elephant
fence
fifteen cents
fourth of July
jump
over
silver
sky

Miss Mary Mack, Mack, Mack
All dressed in black, black, black
With silver buttons, buttons, buttons
All down her back, back, back.
She asked her mother, mother, mother
For fifteen cents, cents, cents
To see the elephants, elephants, elephants
Jump over the fence, fence, fence.
They jumped so high, high, high,
They touched the sky, sky, sky.
And they didn't come back, back, back
Til the fourth of July, -ly, -ly.
And they didn't come down, down, down
Til the fourth of July.

Theme Connections

Animals
Colors
Family
Make-Believe

Did You Know?

❍ Black has two superficially opposite but actually complementary descriptions: Black is the lack of all colors of light, or a combination of multiple colors of pigment.

❍ Black is often a color of mourning. In many cultures, widows and widowers are expected to wear black for a year after the death of their spouses.

❍ Black comedy is a form of comedy dealing with morbid and serious topics. In contrast, the Maasai tribes of Kenya and Tanzania associate the color black with rain clouds, a symbol of life and prosperity.

❍ To say one's accounts are "in the black" means that one is free of debt.

Literacy Links

Oral Language

❍ Ask the children to brainstorm how they might button something that buttons down the back.

❍ Teach the children the American Sign Language sign for *black* (page 123).

Phonological Awareness
○ Point out the *alliteration* in the song (repetition of consonant sounds of two or more words in a row). Challenge children to find rhyming word pairs in the song.
○ Invite the children to brainstorm a list of words that rhyme with black.

Curriculum Connections

Art
○ Provide paper, paintbrushes, and black and silver paint. Encourage the children to paint silver and black pictures.

Blocks
○ Encourage the children to build fences with blocks.

Dramatic Play
○ Fill the center with black clothes for the children to explore. Invite the children to create a black ensemble.

Fine Motor
○ Provide an item of clothing that buttons down the back. Encourage children to first try to button the item by themselves and then ask a friend for help, if needed.

Games
○ Play Who Has the Button? Have children sit in a circle. Choose a child to be IT. Give IT a button. Have the children close their eyes. Help IT choose a friend to give the button to. Invite the children to open their eyes and try to guess who has the button. The child who guesses correctly becomes the next IT.

Gross Motor
○ Provide silver buttons and a decorative box. Encourage the children to toss the buttons into the box.

Language
○ Cut simple advertisements from magazines and laminate them. Give them to the children and provide a crayon for them to use to circle the letter "m".
○ Photocopy, color, cut out, and laminate the Color Rhyming Word Cards (page 115). Challenge the children to find the cards that rhyme with black.

Mary Wore a Red Dress and Henry Wore His Green Sneakers by Merle Peek

Miss Mary Mack by Mary Ann Hoberman

✓ **Special Needs Adaptation:** Children with special needs often have difficulty learning colors. While a child may be able to sort items by color, when asked to point to an object that is a certain color, he may be unable to do so. Adapt this activity by first reviewing basic colors and then by playing a question game with colors. Ask questions, such as, "Who is wearing a red shirt?" or say, "Point to the yellow block."

Math

○ Provide a box of silver buttons and encourage the children to sort them.

○ Give the children pennies. Have them count 15 pennies into a cup. Explain that one penny equals one cent.

Music

○ Sing songs about different Marys, for example, "Mary Had a Little Lamb," "Lazy Mary, Will You Get Up?" and "Mary, Mary, Quite Contrary" (page 101).

Writing

○ Trace around magnetic letters to write *Miss Mary Mack* on sheets of drawing paper. Provide magnetic letters and invite the children to match the letters.

Home Connection

○ Invite the children to look through their clothes at home to find something that buttons down the back.

What Goes Together?

by Pam Schiller

(Tune: Itsy Bitsy Spider)
What goes together?
A button and a coat.
What goes together?
Grass and a goat.
What goes together?
A dog and a flea.
Putting things together,
Good friends like you and me.
(Repeat)

Vocabulary

button
coat
dog
flea
friends
goat
grass
together

Theme Connections

Clothing
Food
Friends

Did You Know?

○ Understanding relationships is fundamental to learning. The definition of intelligence includes the ability to recognize patterns and build relationships from those patterns. The simplest relationship pattern is the pairing of objects that go together.

Literacy Links

Comprehension

○ Teach the children the song "Peanut Butter and Jelly." Discuss the "go together" relationship between peanut butter and jelly.

Oral Language

○ Challenge the children to locate pairs of objects in the classroom that go together such as two puzzle pieces, the table and chairs, and paper and pencils.

○ Display items that go together, such as a toothbrush and toothpaste, a lock and a key, salt and paper, a ball and a glove, and so on. Discuss things that go together.

✓ **Special Needs Adaptation:** Learning how objects relate to each other is an important functional skill for all children, and especially for children with disabilities. A functional skill is defined as a skill that the child will use throughout his life to function in the community. Adapt this activity by selecting no more than four pairs of items that go together. Use real objects and talk about each pair. Look for opportunities during the regular routine to talk about items that go together.

Phonological Awareness

○ Ask children to help identify the rhyming words in the song. Have them brainstorm other words that rhyme with *me*.

Curriculum Connections

Art

○ Fill paint cups with paint and provide a brush for each cup. Invite the children to paint a picture. Remind them of the relationship between each brush and its cup of paint.

Blocks

○ Make milk carton garages by cutting and painting cardboard milk cartons. Give the children the garages and small cars and invite them to park a car in each garage.

Dramatic Play

○ Fill the center with clothing items that go together, such as a pair of socks and shoes, a hat and gloves, and so on. Invite the children to match the items that go together. *Which things are pairs (socks, mittens, gloves) and which things go together (socks and shoes)?*

Fine Motor

○ Provide locks and keys for children to match.
○ Mix up the pieces of several puzzles. Challenge the children to sort the pieces and work the puzzles.

Book Corner

Caps, Hats, Socks, and Mittens by Louise W. Borden

Some Things Go Together by Charlotte Zolotow

Things That Go Together by Vincent Douglas

Wordsong by Bill Martin, Jr.

Games

○ Provide a commercial game with game pieces. Invite the children to play the game. Discuss the relationship between the game pieces. *What happens if a piece gets lost?*

Language

○ Provide a box of items that go together. Ask the children to pair the items.

○ Photocopy, color, cut out, and laminate the Things That Go Together Cards (page 120). Invite the children to pair the cards.

Music

○ Provide clean, empty coffee cans with plastic lids for drums and cardboard tubes from coat hangers for drumsticks. Have the children play their drums to music. Discuss the relationship between the drum and the drumsticks. *Can you play the drum without sticks? What would be different?*

Snack

○ Provide, bread, plastic knives, peanut butter, and jelly. Invite the children to make a sandwich for snack. **Note**: Check for allergies and food sensitivities before serving any food to children.

Home Connection

○ Ask the children to find two things at home that go together and bring them to school the next day. Invite the children to show their items.

Can You Put the Toys Away? by Pam Schiller

Vocabulary

away
end
play
toys

(Tune: Oh, Do You Know the Muffin Man?)
Oh, can you put the toys away,
Toys away, toys away?
Oh, can you put the toys away?
It's time to end our play.
(Repeat)

Theme Connections

Friends
Toys

Did You Know?

○ Children play more intently when they are not overwhelmed by too many choices. Rotate toys. This keeps the amount of toys manageable, and it allows for novelty, which is a great motivator.

○ It is important for teachers to participate actively in this process of putting the toys away so that children acquire the habit through imitation.

○ Songs like "Clean Up" (page 43) and "Can You Put the Toys Away?" help children transition from play activities.

○ For information about cleanup time, see page 43.

Literacy Links

Oral Language

○ Invite the children to create additional verses for the song. Perhaps the verse could describe where toys belong. For example, "put the magnets in their box" or "put the dolly in its bed."

○ Teach the children the American Sign Language sign for *toy* (page 124).

Print Awareness

○ Label some bins where toys belong with both a picture of the item and the printed word. After a while remove the labels and label other toy containers. Too many labels at one time will just be ignored.

Book Corner

Caillou Puts Away His Toys by Joceline Sanschagrin
The Cat in the Hat by Dr. Seuss
Tub Toys by Terry Miller Shannon

Curriculum Connections

Art
○ Encourage the children to draw their favorite classroom toys.

Blocks
○ Trace block shapes to make labels for where blocks go on the shelf. Post the labels and encourage the children to sort the blocks by the labels.

Field Trip
○ Take a trip to a toy store. Call attention to how the toys are organized.

Math
○ Have the children count the number of games and activities in the math center.

Music and Movement
○ Encourage children to pretend to be wind-up toys. Play "Dance of the Toy Soldiers" from *The Nutcracker* and have the children pretend to be dancing soldiers.

Outdoors
○ Discuss the care of outdoor toys. *Where do you put them when you are finished playing with them?*

Writing
○ Invite children to help label bins for toys in the manipulative center either with pictures they cut from catalogs or with their own drawings.

○ For more activities about toys and cleanup time see pages 44-45 in "Clean Up."

Home Connection

○ Talk with families about school procedures and rules surrounding cleanup time. Suggest that children will understand the rules for putting toys away if the rules at home are similar to the rules at school.

Are You Listening?

Vocabulary

boys
circle
down
girls
join
listening
sit

Theme Connections

Me
Parts of the Body
Senses

by Pam Schiller

(Tune: Are You Sleeping?)
Are you listening
Are you listening,
Boys and girls, girls and boys?
Come and join our circle.
Come and join our circle.
Sit right down.
Sit right down.

✔ **Special Needs Adaptation:** Learning to listen is a very important skill for all children to learn. Because some children with special needs have such short attention spans, look for ways to help them participate in the activities related to this song. Try adapting an activity by making it shorter or inviting the child to participate in the activity with a partner. If you have a child in the class who is hearing-impaired, use this song as an additional activity to help build tolerance of individual differences. Explain to the children that a child who is hearing-impaired learns to use other senses to help him know what to do next.

Did You Know?

o Hearing and listening are not the same thing. Hearing is physical. Listening is following and understanding the sound—it is hearing with a purpose.

o An unborn baby begins to hear sounds outside the womb four months before it is born.

o Spiders use the hair on their legs to detect sound.

o Humans have three parts to their ears—the outer ear, the middle ear, and an inner ear. It is the inner ear that processes sound.

o Vibration, a component of sound, is felt by the bones in the inner ear.

Literacy Links

Listening

○ Read the listening story, "Sammy the Seahorse" (pages 104-105). Have the children say, "yippee" when they hear Sammy's name.

○ Ask the children to close their eyes and listen to a sequence of three sounds. Rhythm band instruments work well for this activity because teachers usually have duplicate instruments—a set for you and a set for the child. See if the children can open their eyes and repeat the sequences of sounds they heard using the same three instruments. Play variations of this game by changing the source of the sounds. You can tap a pencil, crumple paper, shake a rattle, and so on.

Listening/Comprehension

○ Tell the children a short story. When you are finished have them describe the way they visualized the key characters and other things in your story.

Oral Language

○ Discuss the use of our ears. Talk about listening for information, listening for directions, and listening for special sounds.

Segmentation

○ Challenge the children to listen for syllables in their names. Encourage them to stand and tap the syllables in their name.

Curriculum Connections

Field Trip

○ Take children on a field trip to a local high school to visit the band or the orchestra. Have them sit in the audience, and then let them sit with the band or orchestra (if it's okay with the band members and/or instructor). What a difference sitting with the group can make!

Games

○ Play Gossip. Sit with the children in a circle. Ask a child to select a word or a phrase and whisper it into the ear of the child sitting on her right. That child then whispers what he heard into the ear of the child to his right. Continue around the circle until all children have heard the word or phrase. Invite the last child to say what he heard out loud. Is it what the first child said? Continue the game for as long as the children show an interest in playing.

○ Play Where's the Sound? The children sit in a circle and close their eyes. Walk to a corner of the room and use a rhythm band instrument to make a sound. See if the children can point in the direction of the sound they hear. (If you don't have a rhythm band instrument, tap a pencil or just whistle.)

○ Play Loud and Soft Hide and Seek. Select a child to be IT. Ask IT to leave the room. Hide a beanbag. When IT returns, tell her you and the children are going to sing a song while she looks for the beanbag. When she is close to where the beanbag is hidden, sing loudly. When she moves farther away, sing more softly.

○ Invite children to play Simon Says. Stress how important it is that they listen carefully.

Listening

○ Record a favorite story and place the tape and a book in the center. Invite the children to listen to the story.

○ Record sounds made by rhythm band instruments. Provide the tape and the instruments. Challenge the children to listen to the tape and identify the instrument that is making the sound.

Math

○ Use a hot glue gun (adult only) or fabric glue to glue three sides of two pieces of 4" square felt together (around the perimeter) to make a bag. Make four more bags. Place one jingle bell in the first bag, two bells in the second bag, three bells in the third, and so on. Use Velcro on the top of each bag to seal it. Invite children to arrange the bags from the loudest to the softest sound. Have the children check the bags to see how many bells are inside each bag.

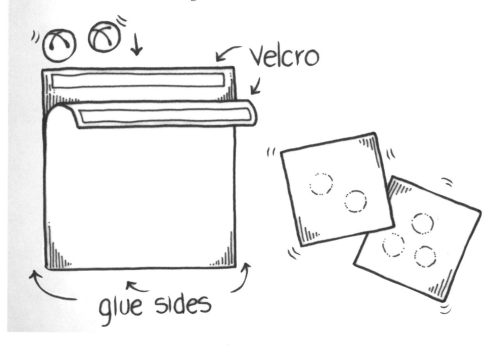

Velcro

glue sides

Book Corner

The Ear Book by Al Perkins

Hearing by Maria Rius

The Listening Walk by Paul Showers

Perk Up Your Ears: Discover Your Sense of Hearing by Vicki Cobb

Polar Bear, Polar Bear, What Do You Hear? by Bill Martin, Jr.

Music and Movement

❍ Sing "The Hokey Pokey." Encourage children to listen carefully to the directions.

Science

❍ Go on a listening walk. Ask the children what they think they might hear. Write their answers in a list and take the list with you when you go outside. Check off the things you hear.

Snack

❍ Provide chunks of cheese, gelatin, graham crackers, and apple slices for snack. Invite the children to decide which snack is the quiet snack and which is the noisy snack.

Home Connection

❍ Encourage the children to teach their family members how to play Simon Says.

Do You Know the Principal? by Pam Schiller

Vocabulary

clean
janitor
librarian
lunchroom staff
neat
office staff
principal
read
school
week

Theme Connection

Community Workers

(Tune: Oh, Do You Know the Muffin Man?)
Oh, do you know the principal,
The principal, the principal?
Oh, do you know the principal?
She runs our school so cool!

Oh, do you know the office staff,
The office staff, the office staff?
Oh, do you know the office staff?
They keep the records straight!

Oh, do you know the janitor,
The janitor, the janitor?
Oh, do you know the janitor?
He keeps things neat and clean!

Oh, do you know the lunchroom staff,
The lunchroom staff, the lunchroom staff?
Oh, do you know the lunchroom staff?
They fix good things to eat!

Oh, do you know the librarian,
The librarian, the librarian?
Oh, do you know the librarian?
She reads to us each week!

Special Needs Adaptation: This song provides an excellent opportunity for children with special needs to learn more about the people who work at their school, and, more importantly, for the school personnel to get to know the child with special needs as a valuable member of the school community. Invite the child with special needs to go with you, and introduce the child by name to school personnel. Invite various people who work at the school into your classroom to talk about what they do in their job. Invite the children in the class to make 'Thank You' pictures for the school personnel who visit your class. Encourage the child with special needs to be part of the team that presents the picture to the school employee.

Did You Know?

○ There are 6.5 million teachers in the United States.

○ Twenty-nine million children participate each month in the national school lunch program. (From the upcoming Statistical Abstract of the United States: 2006.)

○ Almost ten million children from age five to seventeen speak a language other than English at home. These children comprise nearly one in every five children in this age group. Almost seven million speak Spanish at home.

Literacy Links

Oral Language/Print Awareness

○ Make a list of school rules. Discuss the rules and the people who help us follow the rules.

○ Take a tour of your school to visit the different staff members. Have each staff member give a short description of his or her job. Look for signs that identify individual work areas, such as a desk name plate, a sign outside the door, or a nametag.

 English Language Learner Strategy: Have the children introduce themselves, saying "Hi, my name is _____." If the children are just beginning to learn the language, the whole group can say the sentence and the child who is learning English can insert her name.

Print Awareness

○ Print the names of school personnel on chart paper. Point to the names as you sing about them in the song.

Curriculum Connections

Cooking

○ Invite the children to make Celebration Cookies using a rebus (page 107) and invite the school personnel to come join the class for snack time. If that is not possible, deliver a couple of cookies to them.

Dramatic Play

○ Invite the children to pretend to be cafeteria workers. Provide trays, dishes, pretend food, and aprons.

Book Corner

First Day, Hooray by Nancy Roydar
My Teacher's My Friend by P.K. Hallinan
The Principal's New Clothes by Stephanie Calmenson
Will I Have a Friend? by Miriam Cohen

Games

○ Play The Principal Says as you would play Simon Says (page 105).

English Language Learner Strategy: Before playing The Principal Says, review some key vocabulary. For example, touch your head, shoulder, nose, eyes, hair, hands, feet, and toes. Model the actions as you speak and encourage the children to follow. Watch the children to see whether they are following your directions independently. When they are following your directions, they are ready to play The Principal Says. During the game, repeat the instructions and give appropriate wait time for children to respond.

Gross Motor

○ Provide wadded paper balls and a trashcan. Challenge the children to toss the paper into the trashcan. Discuss the job of the custodian. Make sure that children understand that they are helping the custodian when they pick up their own messes.

Language

○ Take the children to the school library and allow them to check out a book.

Library

○ Provide some index cards, pencils, and a few books. Select one child to be the librarian. Encourage the children to pretend they are visiting the library and checking out books. Let the children take turns being the librarian.

Science

○ Ask the school nurse to make a visit to the classroom to measure and weigh the children.

Story Time

○ Invite the principal to read a story at story time. Ask the janitor, office staff, and other school personnel to come to the classroom to read.

Writing

○ Print a few of the school personnel names on chart paper. Provide stick-on nametags and encourage the children to print the names on nametags.

Home Connection

○ Hold an open house and invite all the school personnel to attend. Families will enjoy meeting all the people responsible for their children's school experiences.

Grand Old Duke of York

The grand old Duke of York,
He had ten thousand men.
He marched them up to the top of the hill,
And he marched them down again.
And when they're up, they're up.
And when they're down, they're down.
But when they're only halfway up,
They're neither up nor down.

(Children "act out" the rhyme by standing up, sitting down, and standing halfway up at the appropriate points in the verse.)

✓ **Special Needs Adaptation:** Some of the vocabulary in this song may be too complex for children with language delays. Talk about the words in the song before you introduce it to the entire class. Demonstrate words such as marching, halfway, back and forth, and so on.

Vocabulary

down
duke
grand
halfway
hill
marched
neither
nor
ten thousand
top
up
York

Theme Connections

Nursery Rhymes
Opposites
Spatial Concepts

Did You Know?

○ "The Grand Old Duke of York" is said to be based upon the events of the brief invasion of Flanders by Prince Frederick, Duke of York and Albany. He was commander-in-chief of the British Army during the Napoleonic Wars.

○ The title Grand Duke, used in Western Europe and particularly in Germanic countries for provincial sovereigns, ranks in honor below King but higher than a sovereign Duke or Prince. The feminine form is Grand Duchess. A Grand Duke's territory is called a Grand Duchy.

○ Grand Duke is the usual and established translation of Grand Prince in languages that do not have separate words meaning prince for (1) children of a monarch, and (2) monarch (sovereign or like) princes. The English and French use Grand Duke in this way.

Literacy Links

Oral Language

❍ Discuss *up* and *down*. Discuss other pairs of opposites that are also directional words, such as *forward* and *backward* and *on* and *off*. Ask a volunteer to demonstrate the opposites of *up* and *down* and *forward* and *backward*.

❍ Talk about the title of Duke. Explain to the children that the title is an honor that is below King but higher than a regular Duke or Prince. (See Did You Know?)

❍ Teach the children the American Sign Language signs for *up* and *down* (pages 123-124).

Curriculum Connections

Blocks

❍ Provide an inclined plank and items to roll up and down the plank. Have the children experiment with the items. *Which item rolls down the plank the fastest? Which item is the slowest?*

Discovery

❍ Give the children six raisins and a clear glass filled with ginger ale. Have the children drop the raisins into the glass. The raisins will rise and fall as the bubbles in the ginger ale lift them and then drop them as they reach the surface of the drink and the bubbles pop.

Dramatic Play

❍ Invite the children to crumple newspaper and cover it with fabric to make hills. Provide plastic characters for the children to march up and down the hill.

Fine Motor

❍ Tape a string or a shoelace to a table top or chair back. Have the children sit on the floor and string the beads up the string. What happens?

❍ Provide playdough. Encourage the children to make playdough hills.

Games

❍ Play Duck, Duck, Duke as you would play Duck, Duck, Goose (page 105).

Book Corner

The Grand Old Duke of York by Maureen Roffey

The Grand Old Duke of York by Henry Sowden

❍ Make a Humpty Dumpty Puzzle by cutting an oval shape from construction paper, drawing a face on it, laminating it, and then cutting it into puzzle pieces. Have the children pretend to be the "Duke's men." Tell them that the Duke's men have been called to try to put Humpty Dumpty together. Place the Humpty Dumpty Puzzle pieces inside a plastic egg. Have the children dump out the pieces and try to put Humpty Dumpty together.

Music and Movement

❍ Play marching music and invite the children to march like soldiers.

Outdoors/Science

❍ Hang a pulley from the ceiling. Provide a rope and basket so that the children can use the pulley. Have children show you *up*, *down*, and *halfway up*. **Note**: Supervise closely so that children don't let go of the rope and accidentally hit another child.

Home Connection

❍ Encourage the children to teach "The Grand Old Duke of York" to their families.

MacNamara's Band

Vocabulary

affair
bassoon
colors
conductor
flags
gentry
grand
grand
leader of the band
musicians
procession
puffs
small in number
tootily tootles

Theme Connections

Cultures
Friends
Music

Did You Know?

○ Ireland is an island in the North Atlantic that is divided into the Republic of Ireland and Northern Ireland. The area is internationally known for its folk music, which has remained a vibrant tradition throughout the 20th century, when many traditional forms worldwide lost popularity to pop music.

○ "MacNamara's Band" was Bobby Darin's favorite song when he was a little boy. He could sing the entire song when he was only two years old.

My name is MacNamara.
I'm the leader of a band.
And though we're small in number,
We're the best in all the land.
Of course, I'm the conductor,
And I've often had to play,
With all the fine musicians
That you read about today.

Chorus:
The drums they bang, the cymbals clang,
The horns they blaze away.
McCarthy puffs the old bassoon.
Doyle, the pipes does play.
Hennessey tootily tootles the flute.
The music is something grand.
And a credit to old Ireland's boys
Is MacNamara's Band.

Just now we are a' practicing
For a very grand affair.
It's an annual celebration.
All the gentry will be there.
The girls and boys will all turn out
With flags and colors grand.
And in front of the procession
Will be MacNamara's Band.

(Chorus)

We're the best in all the land.
We're MacNamara's Band!

Literacy Links

Oral Language
○ Provide photos of musical instruments. Discuss the musical instruments mentioned in the song. Categorize the instruments into wind, string, and percussion instruments. Help the children understand that instruments are categorized by how they are played. Wind instruments, which include oboes, flutes, and French horns, are played by blowing into them. String instruments, which include violins, cellos, and violas, are played by drawing a bow across finely-tuned strings. Percussion instruments, which include drums, xylophones, and maracas, are played by striking them with another object (or using your hand).

Phonological Awareness
○ Show the children a pair of cymbals. Clang them together. Ask the children to think of words that describe the sound the cymbals make, such as *crash*, *bam*, *clang*, and so on. Point out that these words are *onomatopoeic* words. Repeat the activity with a drum.

Curriculum Connections

Art
○ Provide paper, paintbrushes, and green tempera paint. Encourage children to paint shamrocks or green pictures.

Construction
○ Give each child an empty toilet paper tube, a rubber band, and a circle of wax paper to make a kazoo. Have the children decorate their toilet paper tubes with markers and then put the wax paper over one end of the tube and secure it with a rubber band. Invite the children to play their kazoos in a parade.

Discovery
○ Pick clover from a lawn or yard (if it is available) and allow children to examine it under a magnifying glass. Remind them that the shamrock is the national symbol for Ireland.

Field Trip
○ Take a field trip to a local high school to visit the band. Categorize the instruments in the band into wind, string, and percussion instruments. *Are there any wind instruments in the band? Why?*

Music and Movement

○ Play Irish music and invite the children to play rhythm band instruments.

✓ **Special Needs Adaptation:** Look for ways that children with physical limitations can participate in the rhythm band. Perhaps they can beat a drum or bells could be attached to their wrists, so they can jingle as the other children play their instruments. If a child can't play a kazoo in the parade, perhaps he could be the band leader.

Social Studies

○ Display a globe. Show the children where Ireland is located on the globe. Tell the children that Ireland is an island. Talk about the weather in Ireland and about Irish customs.

Special Event

○ If you have Irish families in your class, invite them to share information about their heritage. If you have a family or family member who plays musical instruments, have them bring their instrument to class and play it for the children.

○ Invite the children to make and decorate parade hats. Provide marching music and let the children parade through the school playing rhythm band instruments. Remind the children that MacNamara's band leads the parade mentioned in the song.

Writing

○ Print *MacNamara* on chart paper. Then print *MacNamara* on several sheets of drawing paper leaving blanks for the letters "a". Invite the children to fill in the missing letters on the drawing paper after looking at the word on the chart paper.

Home Connection

○ Encourage the children to talk with their families about musical instruments. Suggest that they ask their family member which bands they like best.

Animal Orchestra by Scott Gustafson
Animal Orchestra by Ilo Orleans
Our Marching Band by Lloyd Moss
Song and Dance Man by Karen Ackerman
Zin! Zin! Zin! Violin by Lloyd Moss

Johnny Works With One Hammer

Johnny works with one hammer,
One hammer, one hammer.
Johnny works with one hammer,
Then he works with two.

Additional verses:
Johnny works with two hammers…
Then he works with three.

Johnny works with three
hammers…
Then he works with four.

Johnny works with four hammers…
Then he works with five.

Johnny works with five hammers…
Then he goes to bed!

Vocabulary

five
four
hammer
one
sleep
three
two
works

Did You Know?

❍ Some people believe that "Johnny Works With One Hammer" was inspired by the legend of John Henry.
❍ There are two John Henry's, the actual man and the legend surrounding him. The real John Henry was born a slave, worked as a laborer for the railroads after the Civil War.
❍ John Henry was 6 feet tall and weighed about 200 pounds—a giant in that day. He had a beautiful baritone voice, and was a banjo player.
❍ Information about the legend of John Henry is told mostly through ballads and work songs that were popular with railroad workers during the 19th Century.

Theme Connections

Community Workers
Counting
Numbers

Literacy Links

Oral Language

❍ Sing the song substituting other words for hammer. For example, "Johnny works with one crayon." Sing the song substituting other words for works. For example, "Johnny plays with one truck."
❍ Show the children tools in a toolbox. Discuss each tool. *What is it called? How is it used?* Invite the children to sort the tools by their function. *Which tools are used to tighten or loosen? Which tools are used for putting in nails or screws?*

Book Corner

Changes, Changes by Pat Hutchins
Let's Count by Kelli Chipponeri

Print Awareness

❍ Print one verse of the song on chart paper. Print the number words for each verse on sentence strips. Move your hand under the words as you sing the song. Use the sentence strip number words to substitute into the verse as appropriate. Point out the top-to-bottom and left-to-right progression of the words in the song.

Curriculum Connections

Blocks

❍ Have the children build railroad tracks with the blocks. Help them use the vocabulary associated with railroad tracks, such as crossties, tracks, and crossings.

Construction

❍ Provide lumber scraps and glue. Invite the children to construct a structure.

❍ Provide a hammer, nails, and scrap wood or an old tree stump. Invite the children to hammer the nails into the wood scraps or stump. **Note**: Supervise closely.

Dramatic Play

❍ John Henry was a big man—six feet tall. Provide blankets, pillows, and a tape measure. Challenge the children to create a bed that is big enough for Johnny to sleep in comfortably.

Fine Motor

❍ Provide large nuts and bolts for the children to manipulate.

Math

❍ Print the numerals 1 through 5 on the end of small boxes (checkbook boxes work well). Provide large bolts for the children to count into the numbered boxes.

Home Connection

❍ Suggest that children ask their families to show them were the family toolbox is kept.

Old MacDonald Has a Band

Old MacDonald has a band,
Mi, mi, re, re, do.
And in his band he has some drums,
Mi, mi, re, re, do.
With a rum-tum here, and a rum-tum there.
Here a rum, there a tum,
Everywhere a rum-tum;
Old MacDonald has a band,
The best band in the land.

Additional verses:
…he has some flutes…With a toot-toot…
…he has some fiddles…With a zing-zing…
Old MacDonald has a band,
The best band in the land.

Vocabulary

band
best
drums
fiddles
flutes
rum-tum
toot-toot
zing-zing

Theme Connections

Music
Sounds

Did You Know?

○ Musical instruments are intended to produce sounds that are pleasing when heard in sequence, as in a melody, or at the same time, as in a chord.
○ The *diatonic scale* is comprised of the notes C, D, E, F, G, A, and B or do, re, mi, fa, sol, la, ti. We are so used to this scale that we can sing it naturally, though it is a learned thing.

Literacy Links

Listening

○ Ask the children to shut their eyes. Move to another spot in the room and play a musical instrument. Challenge the children to point in the direction they hear the sound coming from.
○ Ask the children to shut their eyes. Play one of the rhythm band instruments and challenge the children to identify the instrument they hear.

Special Needs Adaptation: Children with special needs can participate in the listening activity, if it is modified for them. Demonstrate how each instrument sounds and say the name of the instrument before asking the children with special needs to shut their eyes. Play each rhythm band instrument and challenge them to identify which instrument they hear. For a child with severe disabilities and/or who is non-verbal, invite the child to play the instrument while other children guess what it is. Participation at any level is very important in building self-confidence in all children, especially those with special needs.

Print Awareness

○ Help the children create a new verse to the song. Perhaps they want to add a fiddle or a tambourine.

○ Print the musical scale on chart paper—do, re, me, fa, sol, la, ti. Sing the scale and have the children repeat it after you. Tell the children that the notes on the musical scale are to music what the alphabet sounds are to reading. Explain that the notes tell musicians which notes to play. Show children notes on sheet music.

Curriculum Connections

Construction

○ Help children make drums using boxes and cans with plastic lids. Provide drumstick, such as cardboard tubes from clothes hangers, dowels, unsharpened pencils, and straws.

○ Help the children make guitars. Provide shallow boxes and rubber bands in different widths. Arrange the rubber bands around the box. Show the children how to strum the rubber bands to create sounds.

Discovery

○ Provide real musical instruments or photos of real instruments in the center for children to explore.

Book Corner

Beat the Drum! by
 Billy Davis
Meet the Orchestra
 by Ann Hayes
Musical Instruments
 From A to Z by
 Bobbie Kalman
Our Marching Band
 by Lloyd Moss
Song and Dance Man
 by Karen
 Ackerman
Zin! Zin! Zin! A Violin
 by Lloyd Moss

Field Trip
○ Take a trip to a high school to visit the band. After the children have listened to the band play as an audience, have them sit beside band members and listen. *How does the listening location change the sound?*

Listening
○ Provide band music and a tape/CD player. Invite the children to listen to the music.

Math
○ Provide a recorder and tape. Encourage the children to tape themselves singing the musical scale. Challenge the children to use a couple of notes and create a pattern, such as do, do, mi; do, do, mi; and so on. Have them practice their patterns and then record them.

Music and Movement
○ Encourage the children to play homemade rhythm instruments, such as two spoons, boxes, pan lids, and empty toilet paper tubes, as they march to marching music.

Writing
○ Print *do, re, mi, fa, sol, la,* and *ti* on chart paper. Provide paper and markers or pencils and encourage the children to copy the notes.

Home Connection

○ Encourage the children to sing the musical scale for their families.

The Color Song

by Pam Schiller

Vocabulary

apples
baby chick
blue
carrots
cherries
eyes
grape juice
grapes
green
jack-o-lantern
leaves
lemonade
orange
oranges
peas
purple
red
strawberries
sun
violet
watermelon
yellow

Theme Connections

Colors
Food

(Tune: Someone's in the Kitchen With Dinah from I've Been Working on the Railroad)

Red is the color for an apple to eat.
Red is the color for cherries, too.
Red is the color for strawberries.
I like red, don't you?

Blue is the color for the big blue sky.
Blue is the color for baby things, too.
Blue is the color of my sister's eyes.
I like blue, don't you?

Yellow is the color of the great big sun.
Yellow is the color for lemonade, too.
Yellow is the color of a baby chick.
I like yellow, don't you?

Green is the color for the leaves on the trees.
Green is the color for green peas, too.
Green is the color of a watermelon.
I like green, don't you?

Orange is the color for oranges.
Orange is the color for carrots, too.
Orange is the color for a jack-o-lantern.
I like orange, don't you?

Purple is the color for a bunch of grapes.
Purple is the color for grape juice, too.
Purple is the color for a violet.
I like purple, don't you?
I like colors don't you?

Did You Know?

❍ Did you ever wonder why you see the colors you do? We see light that bounces off of things around us. When the light enters our eyes, special cells tell our brains about the light. These cells are called *photoreceptors*. Light is made of little bits called *photons*. When the sun shines, trillions and trillions of these little bits of light fall on the earth. The *photons* bounce off of almost everything and some of them enter our eyes, which allow us to see colors.

❍ Different *photons* have different wavelengths. Sunlight contains all the different wavelengths of *photons*. You can see the visible wavelength colors when you look at a rainbow. Raindrops acting as natural prisms produce the colors.

❍ The color red is not "in" an apple. The surface of the apple is reflecting the wavelengths we see as red and absorbing all the rest. An object appears white when it reflects all wavelengths and black when it absorbs them all.

Literacy Links

Comprehension

❍ Ask the children questions about colors. *Which color is your favorite color? Why? What would the world be like if everything was the same color? What if there wasn't a color yellow? What color would the sun be?*

 Special Needs Adaptation: Review the names of colors with the children and show them an object that represents the color you are describing. To help build generalization skills, select three red items, three green items, three yellow items, and so on from the classroom. Invite the children to help you sort the items by color.

Phonological Awareness

❍ Invite children to think of words that rhyme with each color mentioned in the song.

Print Awareness/Oral Language

❍ Challenge the children to brainstorm a list of items that represent each color mentioned in the song.

Curriculum Connections

Art

○ Provide shades of several different colors of construction paper and wallpaper scraps. Invite the children to select one color and make a monochromatic collage.

Discovery

○ Provide prisms and invite the children to make rainbows.

○ Provide a Color Mixing Tube. Place a cork in one end of a two foot section of one-inch plastic tubing (available from the hardware store). Pour five or six drops of red food coloring in the tube and then fill the remainder of the tube with water, leaving an inch from the end of the tube. Drop five or six drops of yellow food coloring into the tube and insert a second cork in the open end of the tube. Have the children turn the tube end over end and watch the colors work their way to the middle of the tube where they will mix. *What color is the water in the middle of the tube?*

Fine Motor

○ Mix blue playdough and yellow playdough. (See page 106 for playdough recipes.) Give each child a small amount of each color of playdough and encourage them to mix the two colors together. *What happens?*

Language

○ Photocopy, color, cut out, and laminate the Color Rhyming Word Cards (page 115). Provide a sheet of red, blue, and black construction paper. Give the children the cards and ask them to find the words that rhyme with each color and place the rhyming word card on top of the color that it rhymes with.

Book Corner

Black on White by Tana Hoban

Brown Bear, Brown Bear, What Do You See? by Bill Martin, Jr.

Color Farm by Lois Ehlert

Colors by Chuck Murphy

Planting a Rainbow by Lois Ehlert

Red, Blue, Yellow Shoe by Tana Hoban

This Little Train by Pam Schiller and Richele Bartkowiak

Music and Movement

❍ Give each child one quarter section of a paper plate, several colors of crepe paper streamers cut in 18" strips, tongue depressors, and glue. Have the children glue streamers onto the rim of the quarter paper plate and then glue the tongue depressor to the point of the paper plate section. When the glue has dried, play music and invite the children to dance with their streamers.

Outdoors

❍ Make your own rainbow. All you need is a sunny day and a garden hose with a spray nozzle. Adjust the spray nozzle so the water is a fine mist. Spray the water high into the air. Have the children stand with the sun behind them and look at the mist from the hose.

❍ Give the children sheets of colored cellophane. Have them hold the cellophane sheets over their heads and look at the colorful shadows they create on the ground.

Snack

❍ Help the children follow the Lemonade Rebus Recipe (page 112).

❍ Suggest that the children follow the Fruit Salad Rebus Recipe (page 109) to make a colorful snack.

 English Language Learner Strategy: Show each fruit that is in the salad. Talk about the skin of each fruit using color vocabulary. Cut each fruit open and talk about the inside using color vocabulary.

Writing

❍ Print color words on index cards. Use the color of marker that matches the word. Provide tracing paper and crayons. Invite the children to trace the words with the color of crayon that matches the color word.

Home Connection

❍ Encourage the children to interview their family members to find out their favorite colors. Have the children bring their information back to school and graph the results. Is one color more popular than the others?

My Hands on My Head

adapted from the version of this song by Jean Feldman

Vocabulary

boca
cabeza
estómago
hand
head
nariz
ojos
orejas
school

Theme Connections

Family
Parts of the Body

My hands on my head—¿Qué es esto?
This is my cabeza. My mamita.
Cabeza, cabeza, la, la, la, la,
That's what I learned in my school. ¡Sí! ¡Sí!

My hands on my eyes—¿Qué son estos?
These are my ojos. My mamita.
Cabeza, ojos, la, la, la, la,
That's what I learned in my school. ¡Sí! ¡Sí!

My hands on my ears—¿Qué son estos?
These are my orejas. My mamita.
Cabeza, ojos, orejas, la, la, la, la,
That's what I learned in my school. ¡Sí! ¡Sí!

Additional verses:
…nose/nariz
…mouth/boca
…stomach/estómago
…feet/pies

Did You Know?

○ Language researchers say that if a child learns 50 words of a second language prior to age five, he or she will develop an ear for the sounds in that language. With an ear for the language they will be able to speak it without an accent or dialect when they receive formal instruction.

○ This song introduces 11 Spanish words.

Literacy Links

Comprehension

○ Make a list of the Spanish words for parts of the body that are introduced in the song. Print the English translation beside each word.

○ Teach the children the original version of "My Hand on My Head" (page 101).

○ Point out that there are many different languages and therefore many different ways to say most words, including using sign language. Teach the children the American Sign Language signs for the parts of the body mentioned in the song (pages 123-124).

Oral Language

○ Teach the children how to count to five in Spanish: uno, dos, tres, quatro, and cinco.

Print Awareness

○ Print *do, re, me, fa, sol, la, ti, do* on chart paper. Tell the children that these words are notes on a scale. Sing the notes. Underline *la*. Explain that *la* is the note that is part of this song. Print *la, la, la, la* on chart paper. Sing a verse of the song. Point to *la, la, la, la* when you reach the appropriate part of the song.

Curriculum Connections

Art

○ Help each child fold a sheet of art paper into three parts and then open it back up. Have the children draw a person that covers the whole sheet of paper. When they are finished ask them to describe the parts of the body that are in the top section, the middle section, and the bottom section of the page.

Construction

○ Invite the children to make Springy Puppets. Give the children two construction paper circles, one 2" in diameter and one 3" in diameter. Fold, accordion style, four 1" wide strips of construction paper, two 8" long and two 12" long. Have the children glue the small circle on the edge of the larger circle to create a body, and then glue the short accordion-folded strips to the sides for arms and the longer strips for legs. Now you have a Springy Puppet. Have the children add facial features and then encourage them to name the parts of the body on their Springy Puppets.

Book Corner

From Head to Toe by Eric Carle

Head, Shoulders, Knees, and Toes by Annie Kubler

My First Spanish Word Book by DK Publications

Toes, Ears, and Nose by Marion Dane Bauer

Fine Motor

○ Place a bowl of beads on the floor. Have the children take off their shoes and try to pick up the beads using the toes on their feet (*pies*).

Games

○ Play *Estómago* (Tummy) Ticklers. Have children lie on the floor on their backs with their heads on someone else's tummy (estómago). Do something silly to make the children start laughing. *What is making their heads jiggle?* This activity should cause contagious laughing.

Gross Motor

○ Use masking tape to create a ten-foot long line on the floor. Challenge the children to walk the line with a beanbag on their *cabezas* (heads).

○ Use masking tape to make a start and a finish line on the floor 6' apart. Place a ping-pong ball on the start line. The children push the ball from the start line to the finish line with their *nariz* (nose).

Music

○ Teach the children simple songs in Spanish like "Jingle Bells" and "Itsy Bitsy Spider."

Home Connection

○ Suggest that the children teach "My Hands on My Head" to their families.

I Like School by Pam Schiller

(Tune: London Bridge Is Falling Down)
I like to sing with my friends,
With my friends, with my friends.
I like to sing with my friends,
Friends like you.

I like to paint and build with blocks,
Build with blocks, build with blocks.
I like to paint and build with blocks.
I like school, don't you?

I like to move and dance with scarves,
Dance with scarves, dance with scarves.
I like to move and dance with scarves.
I like school, don't you?

I like to play on the swings and slide,
Swings and slide, swings and slide.
I like to play on the swings and slide.
I like school, don't you?

I like to sing with my friends,
With my friends, with my friends.
I like to sing with my friends,
Friends like you.

Vocabulary

blocks
build
dance
friends
friends
paint
play
scarves
school
sing
slide
swings
you

Theme Connections

Friends
Me

Did You Know?

○ According to the Census Bureau, in 2003 there were approximately 19.8 million children under the age of 5 in the United States, up 3.1% since 2000. This roughly breaks down to about 4 million children in each age group, or about 8 million 3- and 4-year-olds.

○ Between 1991 and 2001, the percentage of 4-year-olds enrolled in some form of childcare/education program increased by nearly 6%. Enrollment of 3-year-olds has increased by only 0.7%

○ See pages 46 for more School Days facts.

Literacy Links

Comprehension
○ Invite the children to add additional verses to the song.
○ Read "I Like School" (page 104) to the children. Ask questions after the story. *Which school activity do you like best? Which parts of the story sound like something we do in our classroom?*

 English Language Learner Strategy: Tell the story again using props from the classroom and allow the children to handle the props as you retell the story. Ask children to use the props to tell you what comes next in the story.

Oral Language
○ Teach the children the American Sign Language sign for *school* (page 123).

Oral Language/Print Awareness
○ Print *I Like* _____ on chart paper. Have the children offer words to fill in the blank. Make a list of what they like.

Curriculum Connections

Art
○ Provide drawing paper and crayons for the children to illustrate the song.
○ Provide feathers, drawing paper, and tempera paint. Invite the children to paint with the feather.

Blocks
○ Invite the children to build with the blocks. Sit with them and build a structure of your own. Children don't automatically know how to create a structure with the blocks. Watching you will inspire their creativity and expand their understanding of what to do with blocks.

Dramatic Play
○ Provide a few classroom materials, such as puzzles, puppets, paper and crayons, and playdough. Encourage the children to play school.

Field Trip
○ Visit a local park so the children can play on the swings and slides.

Book Corner

Hurray for Pre-K! by
Ellen B. Senisi

Listening

❍ Provide a tape recorder. Suggest that the
children sing a song. Record the song and
then play it back so the children can
hear their song.

Music and Movement

❍ Play music and invite the children
to take off their shoes and dance in their
socks.

Writing

❍ Print *I like* _____ on a sheet of paper. Provide index cards with
different words written on them, such as *mommy*, *swinging*, *singing*, and
playing. Add rebus drawings to the cards to help the children know what
the word says. Invite the children to use different cards to finish the
sentence.

Home Connection

❍ Send drawing paper home with each child. Have them ask their adult
family members to draw a picture of their favorite school memory.

B-B-B-Bubbles by Pam Schiller

Vocabulary

adore
beauty
blow
bubbles
few
more

(Tune: K-K-K-Katy)
B-B-B-Bubbles, beautiful bubbles
Blow just a few and you'll want more.
B-B-B-Bubbles, beautiful bubbles
Oh, it's beautiful b-b-bubbles we adore.

Theme Connections

Me
Sounds

Did You Know?

○ Bubbles are made of air trapped inside a hollow liquid ball. The colors visible in bubbles come from light reflecting on the surface of the bubbles. Bubbles float up because warm air is lighter than cold air. If the air blown into the bubble is warmer than the air around it, the bubble will float up.

○ There are many great bubble recipes. Try a few to find a bubble recipe that works for you. The type of dishwashing liquid you use, the weather outside, and the type of water you use can all affect bubble quality. Some mixtures produce longer-lasting bubbles if placed in the refrigerator for a few minutes or if allowed to stand for a day or two before using. Using more detergent than water creates giant bubbles, and adding glycerin or sugar slows down water evaporation that causes bubbles to pop.

○ See page 94 in "Bubbles in the Air" for additional information about bubbles.

Literacy Links

Oral Language

○ Invite the children to talk about experiences they have had with bubbles.
○ Teach the children the American Sign Language sign for *bubble* (page 123).

Phonological Awareness

○ Print *B-B-B Bubbles* on chart paper. Have the children make the /b/ sound with you. Print a couple of the children's names on the chart paper with the beginning sound letter repeated at the beginning of each name in the same way as in "B-B-B Bubbles." For example, Madison will be M-M-M-Madison.

○ Challenge children to think of words that rhyme with *bubble*.

Curriculum Connections

Art

○ Provide tempera paint, paper, and large-size bubble wrap. Invite the children to make bubble prints by dipping the bubble wrap into the tempera paint and then pressing it onto their paper.

Discovery

○ Put ¼ cup baking soda in a clear container. Add 1 cup vinegar. The mixture of vinegar and baking soda will bubble. It's making carbon dioxide. Blow some bubbles into the container and have children watch how they float on the carbon dioxide. The bubbles are floating where the carbon dioxide and air meet. The carbon dioxide stays at the bottom of the bowl because it is denser than the air in the bowl. The bubbles float on top of the carbon dioxide because they are filled with air and the air is less dense than the carbon dioxide. Try the experiment again. This time mix ¼ cup baking soda and 1 cup lemon juice. What happens?

○ Provide a Bubble Tube. Place a cork in one end of a two foot section of one-inch plastic tubing (available from the hardware store). Fill the plastic tubing with bubble mixture, leaving an inch from the end of the tube. Insert a second cork in the open end of the tube. Have the children turn the tube end over end and watch the bubbles work their way up and down the tube.

Fine Motor

○ Show children how to soap up their hands and blow a bubble through their fist. First, lather your hands with soapy water, especially your thumb and index finger. Then make a loose fist and blow through the circle made by your thumb and index finger.

Book Corner

A My Name Is Alice
by Jane Bayer
Bubble Bubble by
Mercer Mayer
*Clifford Counts
Bubbles* by
Norman Birdwell
*Little Blue and Little
Yellow* by Leo
Lionni

Outdoors

○ Blow bubbles. Call out directions for the children to follow. For example, pop a bubble with your head, with your elbow, with your wrist, and so on.

✔ **Special Needs Adaptation:** For children with motor skills challenges or those who can't blow bubbles, try to find an alternative way for them to participate, such as asking the child to hold the bubble wand while a friend blows the bubbles. If a child is unable to pop the bubbles with his body parts, invite him to join in the activity but allow his bubbles to pop naturally.

Science

○ Place a large sheet of butcher paper on the floor or outdoors on the sidewalk. Add blue food color to a small container of bubbles and yellow to another. Let the children blow bubbles. As the bubbles pop onto the paper they make blue or yellow circles. Children will discover green bubbles when the blue and yellow bubble solutions mix.

Snack

○ Serve a bubbly drink such as ginger ale, ginger ale mixed with orange sherbet, or juice mixed with seltzer or sparkling water.

Special Event

○ Have the children blow bubbles for a younger class or younger siblings.

Home Connection

○ Send bubble mixture (see page 106) home with the children so they can show their families how to blow bubbles through their fist.

Stop, Drop, and Roll

by Richele Bartkowiak

(Tune: Three Blind Mice)
Stop, drop, and roll.
Stop, drop, and roll.
If ever your clothes catch on fire,
Stop, drop, and roll.
Remember this rule,
This golden safety rule.
If ever your clothes catch on fire,
Stop, drop, and roll.

Vocabulary

catch on fire
clothes
drop
golden
roll
rule
safety
stop

Theme Connections

Community Workers
Health and Safety

Did You Know?

○ Fire is the third leading cause of accidental deaths in the United States.
○ Eighty percent of all fire deaths occur in the home. A fire can engulf a house in a matter of minutes.
○ Most fires can be prevented. Smoke detectors more than double the chance of surviving a fire.
○ Most fatal home fires occur at night, while people sleep. Fire produces toxic gases and smoke that numbs the senses. If you are asleep, or become disoriented by toxic gases, you may not even realize that there is a fire.

Literacy Links

Letter Knowledge
○ Print *Stop, Drop, and Roll* on chart paper. Ask the children to identify the letters in each word. *Which letter appears in all three words?*

Oral Language
○ Teach the children the American Sign Language sign for *fire* (page 123).

○ Talk about fire safety. For example, not playing with matches, staying away from open heaters, and so on. Teach the children how to dial 911. Practice how to Stop, Drop, and Roll.

 English Language Learner Strategy: Allow the children who are not proficient in English to pantomime the action while you describe their actions.

Curriculum Connections

Blocks

○ Provide a variety of weighted cans for children to roll. Fill coffee cans with blocks to create different weights. Make a masking tape line on the floor and challenge the children to roll the cans along the line. *Do heavy cans roll easier than light cans?*

Cooking

○ Make cookies for firefighters. Use the rebus recipe for Celebration Cookies (page 107).

Field Trip

○ Visit a fire station. Discuss fire safety with the firefighters. Bring the cookies that you made (see above).

Fine Motor

○ Invite the children to play Drop the Bag. Provide coffee cans and beanbags. Encourage the children to drop the beanbags into the coffee cans.

Games

○ Invite children to play Stop and Go. Give the children a direction. They begin the activity when you say "go" and stop it when you say "stop." For example, if the direction is "jump up and down," they jump up and down when you say "go" and stop jumping up and down when you say "stop."

Gross Motor

○ Have the children practice Stop, Drop, and Roll. Make a drop line on the floor with masking tape. Instruct the children to roll at least four times. Remind them that in real life they would roll until their clothes

Book Corner

Fire! Fire! by Gail
    Gibbons
*"Fire! Fire!" Said Mrs.
    McGuire* by Bill
    Martin, Jr.
Fire Safety by Pati
    Myers Gross
*No Dragons for Tea:
    Fire Safety for
    Kids* by Jean
    Pendziwol
Stop, Drop, and Roll
    by Margery
    Cuyler

were no longer on fire. Provide measuring tapes so the children can see how far they roll in four rolls. *How much further would they roll if they rolled one more time?*

❍ Make a pathway by placing two 10′ lines of masking tape four feet a part on the floor. Challenge the children to roll between the lines. *Why is it not as easy as it sounds?*

Writing

❍ Print *Stop, Drop, and Roll* on chart paper. Have the children copy the rule onto drawing paper and then draw an illustration to create a fire safety poster.

Home Connection

❍ Suggest that families prepare a fire escape plan for their homes. Most fires happen in homes and generally at night when people are sleeping. The first rule of survival is to have a plan for escape. Make sure families are aware of the importance of smoke detectors.

Rhyme Time

Vocabulary

can
fan
man
pan
ran
rhyme
tan
time

Theme Connection

Sounds

(Tune: The Addams' Family)
Rhyme time (*snap twice*),
Rhyme time (*snap twice*),
Rhyme time, rhyme time, rhyme time (*snap twice*).

Verse:
There's can and there's pan.
There's fan and there's ran.
There's man and there's tan.
The "-an" family.

Additional verses:
Pet, jet, vet, net, let, set…
Like, hike, bike, mike, trike, pike…
Pot, dot, hot, not, lot, got…
Sat, mat, hat, cat, bat, pat…
Book, look, cook, hook, took, nook…

Did You Know?

○ One of the most accurate predictors of reading success is the child's ability to discriminate sounds. Fundamental to this ability is the ability to identify rhyming words.

○ Rhyming words occur less frequently in Latin-based languages.

Literacy Links

Letter Knowledge/Phonological Awareness

○ Print one of the word families on chart paper. Call attention to the beginning letter in each word. Help children recognize that all that changes for each word is the first letter.

Phonological Awareness

❍ Give the children a letter and have them use the letter to substitute for the first letter of their name. For example, if you name the letter "F", children will change their name in this way. Pam becomes Fam, Kathy becomes Fathy, and Juan becomes Fuan.

❍ Invite the children to follow the directions in "Say and Touch."

Say and Touch
Say "red," and touch your head.
Say "sky," and touch your eye.
Say "bear," and touch your hair.
Say "hear," and touch your ear.
Say "south," and touch your mouth.
Say "rose," and touch your nose.

❍ Give children another rhyme pattern and encourage them to add a verse to the song.

✓ **English Language Learner Strategy:** Sing "Clap, Tap, Snap" to the tune of "London Bridge Is Falling Down." Help the children identify the rhyming words. Discuss the "ap" family and then sing the song again.

Clap, Tap, Snap by Pam Schiller
Little hands go clap, clap, clap,
Clap, clap, clap,
Clap, clap, clap.
Little hands go clap, clap, clap
Now put 'em in your lap.

Little hands go snap, snap, snap…
Little toes go tap, tap, tap…
Now I'll take a nap.

Curriculum Connections

Art

❍ Encourage the children to create a pattern of spots and dots. Show the children how to use crayons or markers to make dots (touch crayon or marker to paper) and spots (larger dots).

Blocks

○ Invite the children to play Sock the Blocks. Make paper bag blocks by stuffing paper grocery bags three-quarters full with crumpled newspaper and then folding the top over and taping with duct tape or masking tape. Invite the children to stack the blocks and sock them (hit the blocks with their hands) until they have all fallen.

Games

○ Play Don't Let the Ball Fall. Have the children stand in a circle. They toss a ball around the circle, being careful not to let the ball fall. If someone drops the ball she must do an action for her friends to copy. After everyone has copied the action, the child who dropped the ball starts it around the circle again.

Language

○ Photocopy, color, cut out, and laminate the Color Rhyming Words Card (page 115). Give the children sheets of blue, red, and black construction paper. Ask them to determine which cards feature an item that rhymes with the color.

○ Provide magnetic letters and encourage the children to make up words in the "at" family.

Music and Movement

○ Play rock and roll music and invite the children to "rock in their socks."

Snack

○ Have the children follow the Cracker Stacker Rebus Recipe (page 108) to make their snack.

✓ **English Language Learner Strategy:** Take photo of the children making their Cracker Stackers. Tape record each step. Place the tape and photos in the Listening Center and have English proficient children pair with English language learners to sequence the photos as they listen to the tape.

Home Connection

○ Ask families to send a pair of rhyming objects to school, such as a sock and a rock or a shoe and glue. Or they can send pictures of two things that rhyme. Encourage children to share their rhyming word pairs.

Down by the Bay by Raffi
Green Eggs and Ham by Dr. Suess
One Fish, Two Fish, Red Fish, Blue Fish by Dr. Suess

SONGS AND ACTIVITIES

Bubbles in the Air

by Pam Schiller

(Tune: If You're Happy and You Know It)
Bubbles in the air, in the air.
Bubbles in the air, in the air.
Bubbles in the air
Look, there are bubbles
    everywhere!
Bubbles in the air, in the air.

Bubbles in my hair, in my hair.
Bubbles in my hair, in my hair.
Bubbles in my hair and
I don't even care.
Bubbles in my hair, in my hair.

Bubbles way up there, way up there.
Bubbles way up there, way up there.
Stretch and reach them if you can
Knock them down with your hand.
Bubbles way up there, way up there.

Bubbles in the air, in the air.
Bubbles in the air, in the air.
Bubbles in the air
Pop them if you dare.
Bubbles in the air, in the air.

Vocabulary

air
bubbles
dare
everywhere
hair
knock
reach
stretch
there
up

Theme Connections

Me
Spatial Concepts

Did You Know?

○ You can blow good bubbles with any dish soap if you dilute it with a little water. Adding glycerin makes the bubbles last longer and the colors brighter!

○ The colors in the bubbles come from interference between light that reflects from the inside of the bubbles and the outside of the bubbles.

○ For more bubble information see page 85 in "B-B-B-Bubbles."

Literacy Links

Letter Knowledge
○ Print *bubble* on chart paper. Ask the children to identify the letters. *Which letter is repeated several times?*

Oral Language
○ Blow bubbles. Encourage a volunteer to pick a bubble and describe its movements. For example, the bubble is going up, down, high, low, left, right, and so on.
○ Teach the children the American Sign Language sign for *bubble* (page 123).

Curriculum Connections

Art
○ Add tempera paint to bubble mixture and stir the mixture with a beater until you have bubbles on top of the mixture. Give the children paper to press on top of the bubble container to make bubble prints.

Discovery
○ Make two holes in the lid of a plastic sour cream or yogurt container. Insert a straw through one of the holes and leave the other hole open. Pour bubble solution in the cup and cover. Invite the children to blow out through the straw and watch the bubbles pour out over the top of the cup and down the sides.
○ Provide a Bubble Tube. Place a cork in one end of a two feet section of one-inch plastic tubing (available from the hardware store). Fill the plastic tubing with bubble mixture, leaving an inch from the end of the tube. Insert a second cork in the open end of the tube. Have the children turn the end over end and watch the bubble work their way up and down the tube.

Special Needs Adaptation: Several of the following activities may be difficult for a child with special needs to do independently. Use these activities as an opportunity to encourage collaboration and peer buddy interaction. Select a peer buddy and invite her to work with the child with special needs to complete the activity together. For future activities, when the child with special needs is more comfortable with a peer buddy, he may want to select a peer buddy by himself.

SONGS AND ACTIVITIES

Book Corner

Benny's Big Bubble
    by Jane
    O'Connor
Bubble Bubble by
    Mercer Mayer
*Over, Under,
    Through, and
    Other Spatial
    Concepts* by
    Tana Hoban
*Pop! A Book About
    Bubbles* by
    Kimberly
    Brubaker Bradley

Fine Motor

❍ Give the children large-size bubble wrap to pop.

Music

❍ Invite the children to sing bubble songs like "The Bubble Song" and "The Bubbles Soar Over the Playground" (page 100).

Outdoors

❍ Blow bubbles. Challenge the children to work together to keep a bubble floating in the air.

Outdoors/Games

❍ Provide bubble solution and wands to each child. Have the children catch a bubble on their wands and then see how many steps they can take with the bubble before it pops.

Science

❍ Show the children some bubble "magic." Wet your hands with bubble solution and then catch a bubble in your hand. It does not pop! Wet the end of a straw with bubble mixture and stick it in a bubble. The bubble does not pop! Blow a bubble so it lands on a table and invite the children to observe the colors in the bubble. (**Note**: Before blowing bubbles, spread a thin layer of bubble mixture on the table to prevent bubbles from popping when they land on the table.

Snack

❍ Provide a bubbly drink for snack. Mix three cups of grape juice with one quart of ginger ale.

❍ See pages 86-87 for additional bubble activities.

Home Connection

❍ Encourage the children to show their families how dish soap can be used for making bubbles.

Happy Faces by Pam Schiller

Vocabulary

faces
fun
giggling
play
smiling
today
work

(Tune: Jingle Bells)
Smiling faces, happy faces
Giggling all around.
Oh, what fun we'll have today
As we work and play.
Ha-ha, he-he-he,
Ha-ha-ha, ho-ho-hey!
Oh, what fun we'll have today
As we work and play.

Theme Connections

Friends
Me

Did You Know?

○   Laughing is good for you. It increases the endorphins in your blood stream, which protects your immune system and also boosts your memory.

○ On average, children laugh 400 times per day and adults only 15 times per day. (Diggs, T.S. "Laughter: Is it healthy?" *Magic Stream Journal: A Guide to Emotional Wellness*, Issue 6, Fall 1997.)

○ There are two aspects to the face—the genetic structure (the color of the eyes, shape of the jaws, lips, nose, and so on) and the nuances of the face (facial expressions).

○ There are over 7,000 expressions that the human face can make, but we normally only make a few hundred. Each expression is linked to different parts of the brain.

○ The modern skill of reading facial expressions owes a lot to Paul Ekman. As a young psychologist growing up in San Francisco in the 1960s, Ekman began to study the human face, including its features and expressions. His quest led him around the world several times and ultimately resulted in the formation of the Facial Action Coding System, or FACS, a detailed set of rules for reading and interpreting faces, including a description of 3,000 of the most common facial expressions and when they're used. FACS has been used by everyone from research groups studying behavioral disorders to the animators of Toy Story and Shrek movies.

Literacy Links

Oral Language

○ Give children a mirror and have them look at their faces. Encourage them to describe what they see. *What color are your eyes? Are you smiling? Do you have a serious look on your face? What happens to your eyes when you smile? What happens to your mouth?*

○ Teach the children the American Sign Language signs for *face* and *happy* (page 123).

○ Discuss the value of laughing with the children. Explain that laughing and giggling helps them stay healthy and remember things better.

✓ **Special Needs Adaptation:** Learning to express emotion is very difficult for some children with special needs. Invite the children to help make a list of things that make them laugh. Talk about when it is appropriate to laugh and when it is not. Sometimes, children with certain types of disabilities will laugh inappropriately, such as when another child falls down. Talk about how much fun it is to laugh, and role play situations when it is okay to laugh.

Print Awareness

○ Ask the children to brainstorm a list of things that make them happy. Print their list on chart paper. Discuss the purpose of making list. *What other things might we make a list for?* (grocery list, to do list, and so on)

Print Awareness/Phonological Awareness

○ Invite the children to brainstorm a list of words used for laughing like "ha-ha-ha" and "he-he-he." Write their words on chart paper. Explain that these words are *onomatopoeic* words, words that sound like the sound they are describing.

Curriculum Connections

Construction

○ Invite the children to make Happy Face Puppets. Provide six-inch paper plates, markers, yarn, wiggle eyes, and a tongue depressor. Have the children draw or glue a happy face on the plate, add yarn for hair, and then attach to the tongue depressor to make a Happy Face Puppet. Encourage the children to sing the song, "Happy Faces" (page 97) with their puppets.

Book Corner

Fine Motor
○ Have the children look through magazines for happy faces. Encourage them to cut out the faces and glue them to a sheet of paper to make a Happy Face Collage.
○ Provide playdough, yarn, and wiggle eyes. Suggest that the children shape a happy face with the playdough.

Games
○ Invite the children to play You Can't Make Me Laugh. Select one child to be IT. Have the children sit in a circle with IT in the middle. Invite IT to do silly things that might make his classmates laugh. The first child to laugh becomes the new IT.
○ Invite the children to play Tummy Ticklers (page 81 in "My Hands On My Head").

Language
○ Draw happy faces on index cards. Make two blue faces, two red faces, two yellow faces, and two green faces. Invite the children to turn the cards face down and play a game of Happy Face Concentration.

Listening
○ Provide a tape recorder. Encourage the children to tape themselves laughing and then listen to the tape.

Snack
○ Encourage the children to follow the Happy Face Pizza Rebus Recipe (page 111) to make a happy snack.

Writing
○ Trace around magnetic letters to write *happy* on several large index cards. Encourage the children to match magnetic letters to the outlines you made on the cards.
○ Print *ha-ha-ha* and *he-he-he* on chart paper and encourage the children to use crayons to copy the words on their own paper.

Home Connection

○ Encourage the children to talk with their families about things that make them laugh.

Baby Faces by Margaret Miller

Giggle Belly by Page Sakelaris

Giggle, Giggle, Quack by Doreen Cronin

Toes Have Wiggles, Kids Have Giggles by Harriet Ziefert

SONGS AND ACTIVITIES

More Learning and Fun

Songs

The Bubble Song
One little, two little, three little bubbles,
Four little, five little, six little bubbles,
Seven little, eight little, nine little bubbles,
Ten little bubbles go pop, pop, pop.

Pop those, pop those, pop those bubbles,
Pop those, pop those, pop those bubbles,
Pop those, pop those, pop those bubbles,
Ten little bubbles go pop, pop, pop.

The Bubbles Soar Over the Playground
by Pam Schiller
(Tune: My Bonnie Lies Over the Ocean)
The bubbles soar over the playground,
The bubbles blow high in the tree,
The bubbles dance gaily around me,
Oh, dance back sweet bubbles to me.

Dance back, dance back
Dance back sweet bubbles to me, to me.
Dance back, dance back
Dance back sweet bubbles to me.

Good Morning
(Tune: If You're Happy and You Know It)
Good morning, (child's first and last name).
How are you?
Good morning, (child's first and last name).
How are you?
How are you this special day?

We're glad you came to play.
Good morning, (child's first and last name).
How are you?

Good Morning to You (Version 2)
Good morning to you.
Good morning to you.
We're all in our places
With sunshiny faces,
And this is the way
To start a new day!

Good morning to you.
Good morning to you.
Our day is beginning,
There's so much to do
So good morning, good morning,
Good morning to you!

Good Morning to You (Version 3)
Good morning, good morning,
 good morning to you.
Good morning, good morning,
 good morning to you.
Our day is beginning, there's so much to do,
So, good morning, good morning,
 good morning to you.

The Mulberry Bush
Here we go 'round the mulberry bush, (hold
 hands and walk in circle)
The mulberry bush, the mulberry bush.
Here we go 'round the mulberry bush
So early in the morning.

This is the way we wash our clothes,
   (suit actions to words)
Wash our clothes, wash our clothes.
This is the way we wash our clothes
So early Monday morning.

This is the way we iron our clothes. . .
   Tuesday morning.
This is the way we scrub the floors. . .
   Wednesday morning.
This is the way we sew our clothes. . .
   Thursday morning.
This is the way we sweep the house. . .
   Friday morning.
This is the way we bake our bread. . .
   Saturday morning.
This is the way we go to church. . .
   Sunday morning.

In the Merry, Merry Month of May

by Stephen Foster
We roamed the fields and river sides,
When we are young and gay;
We chased the bees and plucked the flowers,
In the merry, merry month of May.

Chorus:
Oh, yes, with ever changing sports,
We whiled the hours away;
The skies were bright,
Our hearts were light,
In the merry, merry month of May.

Lazy Mary, Will You Get Up?

Lazy Mary, will you get up?
Will you get up? Will you get up?
Lazy Mary, will you get up
This cold and frosty morning?

Mary Had a Little Lamb

Mary had a little lamb,
Little lamb, little lamb.
Mary had a little lamb,
Its fleece was white as snow.

And everywhere that Mary went,
Mary went, Mary went,
Everywhere that Mary went
The lamb was sure to go.

Mary, Mary, Quite Contrary

Mary, Mary, quite contrary
How does your garden grow?
With silver bells and cockleshells
And pretty maids all in a row.

My Hand on My Head

My hand on my head, (place hand on head)
What have I here? (open arms palm up)
This is my top-notcher, (point to head)
Mamma, my dear.
Top-notcher, top-notcher, (point to head again)
Dickie, dickie, doo. (knock on head)
That's what I learned in my school.
   (shake index finger)
Boom! Boom!

My hand on my brow, (place hand on brow)
What have I here? (open arms palm up)
This is my sweat boxer, (point to forehead)
Mamma, my dear.
Sweat boxer, topnotcher, (point to head and then
   forehead)
Dickie, dickie, doo. (knock on head)
That's what I learned in my school.
   (shake index finger)
Boom! Boom!

(Continue adding body parts and suit hand
   motions to words.)
Eye—eye blinker
Nose—nose blower
Mouth—food grinder
Chin—chin chopper
Heart—chest ticker
Stomach—bread basket
Knee—knee bender
Toe—pedal pusher

This Is the Way We Brush Our Teeth

by Pam Schiller

(Tune: The Mulberry Bush)

This is the way we brush our teeth,
Brush our teeth, brush our teeth.
This is the way we brush our teeth,
Every night and morning.

Move your brush both up and down,
Up and down, up and down.
Move your brush both up and down
Every night and morning.

Brush in the back and in the front,
In the back, in the front.
Brush in the back and in the front,
Every night and morning.

Floss between all your teeth,
All your teeth, all your teeth.
Floss between all your teeth
Every night and morning.

Poems and Chants

Good Morning

I say good morning to my mommy,
Good morning to my daddy,
Good morning to the sun in the sky.
"Good morning."
Good morning to my kitty,
Good morning to my dog,
Good morning to my birdie in his cage.
"Good morning."
I say, "Good morning, good morning,"
To everything in sight. And when I am finished,
It's time to say, "Good night."

Good Night and Good Morning

A fair little girl sat under a tree
Sewing as long as her eyes could see;
She smoothed her work and folded it right,
And said, "Dear work, good night, good night."

Such a number of rooks flew over her head,
Crying, "Caw! Caw!" on their way to bed,
She said, as she watched their curious flight,
"Little black things, good night, good night."

The horses neighed and the oxen lowed,
The sheep's bleat, bleat, came over the road,
All seeming to say, with a quiet delight,
"Dear little girl, good night, good night!"

She did not say to the sun Good night,
Though she saw him there like a ball of light,
For she knew he had God's time to keep,
All over the world and never could sleep.

In the Merry Month of May

In the merry month of May
When green leaves begin to spring,
Little lambs do skip like fairies
Birds do couple, build and sing.

Fingerplays

April Clouds

Two little clouds one April day (*hold both
hands in fists*)
Went sailing across the sky. (*move fists towards
each other*)
They went so fast that they bumped their heads
(*bump fists together*)
And both began to cry. (*point to eyes*)

The big round sun came out and said, (*make circle
with arms*)
"Oh, never mind, my dears,
I'll send all my sunbeams down (*wiggle fingers
downward like rain*)
To dry your fallen tears."

Five Little Snowmen

Five little snowmen happy and gay, (*hold up five
fingers and move one for each snowman*)
The first one said, "What a nice day!"
The second on said, "We'll cry no tears,"
The third one said, "We'll stay for years."
The fourth one said, "But what happens in May?"
The fifth one said, "Look, we're melting away!"
(*hold hands out like saying all gone*)

Where Is Thumbkin?

(Tune: Frère Jacques)
Where is thumbkin? (*hands behind back*)
Where is thumbkin?
Here I am. Here I am. (*bring out right thumb,
then left*)
How are you today, sir? (*bend right thumb*)
Very well, I thank you. (*bend left thumb*)
Run away. Run away. (*put right thumb behind
back, then left thumb behind back*)

Other verses:
Where is Pointer?
Where is Middle One?
Where is Ring Finger?
Where is Pinky?
Where are all of them?

Stories

Mrs. Wiggle and Mrs. Waggle
Action Story

This is Mrs. Wiggle (*hold up right hand, make a fist
but keep the thumb pointing up; wiggle thumb*)
and this is Mrs. Waggle (*hold up left hand, make a
fist but keep the thumb pointing up; wiggle
thumb*). Mrs. Wiggle and Mrs. Waggle live in
houses on top of different hills and three hills apart
(*put thumbs inside fists*).

One day, Mrs. Wiggle decided to visit Mrs.
Waggle. She opened her door (*open right fist*),
pop, stepped outside (*raise thumb*), pop, and
closed her door (*close fist*), pop. Then she went
down the hill and up the hill, and down the hill
and up the hill, and down the hill and up the hill
(*move right hand up and down in a wave fashion
to go with text*).

When she reached Mrs. Waggle's house, she
knocked on the door—knock, knock, knock (*tap
right thumb against left fist*). No one answered. So
Mrs. Wiggle went down the hill and up the hill,
and down the hill and up the hill, and down the
hill and up the hill to her house (*use wave motion
to follow text*). When she reached her house, Mrs.
Wiggle opened the door (*open right fist*), pop,
went inside (*place thumb in palm*), pop, and
closed the door (*close fist*), pop.

The next day Mrs. Waggle decided to visit Mrs.
Wiggle. She opened her door (*open left fist*), pop,
stepped outside (*raise thumb*), pop, and closed his
door (*close fist*), pop. Then she went down the hill
and up the hill, and down the hill and up the hill,
and down the hill and up the hill (*move left hand
up and down in a wave fashion to go with text*).

When she reached Mrs. Wiggle's house she
knocked on the door—knock, knock, knock (*tap
left thumb against right fist*). No one answered. So
Mrs. Waggle went down the hill and up the
hill, and down the hill and up the hill, and

down the hill and up the hill to her house (use wave motion to follow text). When she reached her house, Mrs. Waggle opened the door (open left fist), pop, went inside (place thumb in palm), pop, and closed the door (close fist), pop.

The next day Mrs. Wiggle (shake right fist) decided to visit Mrs. Waggle, and Mrs. Waggle (shake left fist) decided to visit Mrs. Wiggle. So they opened their doors (open both fists), pop, stepped outside (raise thumbs), and closed their doors (close fists), pop. They each went down the hill and up the hill, and down the hill and up the hill (wave motion to follow text), and they met on top of the hill.

They talked and laughed and visited (wiggle thumbs) until the sun went down. Then they went down the hill and up the hill, and down the hill and up the hill, to their own homes (wave motion with both hands to text). They opened their doors (open fists), pop, went inside (tuck thumbs inside), pop, closed their doors (close fists), pop, and went to sleep (place your head on your hands).

I Like School by Pam Schiller

I like school,
I like it a lot,
It's my favorite place
Believe it or not.

I love blowing bubbles,
I love all the toys.
I love the quiet,
And I love the noise.

I love painting with feathers.
And building with blocks,
Reading good books,
And dancing in socks.

Outdoor time is always fun,
Running and hiding
And laughing with friends,
    While swinging and sliding.

My teacher loves me,
I know that it's true.
We smile and laugh
The whole day through.

I'm a (insert name of school) kid
It's plain to see
'Cause I'm just as happy
As a kid can be.

Sammy the Seahorse Listening Story

Sammy is a seahorse. He lives in the ocean. He loves the ocean. It is the only home he has ever known. However, Sammy dreams of being a real horse. He wants to be a rodeo horse.

You might wonder how a little seahorse in the middle of the ocean even knows about rodeo horses. Well, since Sammy was a baby seahorse, his daddy has told him rodeo stories. You see, there are lots of rodeos in Texas, and Sammy's daddy once lived in an aquarium in San Antonio, Texas. Sammy's daddy loved to hear the people talk about rodeos, especially the rodeo horses. Of course, all of that was a long time ago before the people at the aquarium decided to let Sammy's daddy return to the ocean.

Early every morning, Sammy plays in the waves, pretending to be a bucking rodeo horse. Around noontime, he heads home for lunch, pretending to ride herd on a school of fish. He thinks the fish make great cattle. The fish ignore him, but he doesn't care. He heads on down to the bottom of the ocean and nibbles on seaweed, pretending all the while that it is a bale of hay.

After lunch, Sammy darts in and out of the coral pretending to be a cutting horse carrying a rider around the barrels. He has gotten really good at moving quickly in and out of tight places.

When a school of brightly colored parrotfish

comes along, Sammy pretends that they are rodeo clowns. He likes to pretend that they are rescuing him from the horns of an angry bull.

Sammy knows he will never get to be in a real rodeo, but that's all right with him. He loves living in the ocean and wouldn't want to leave it. Besides, he has lots of fun just pretending in his world of make-believe.

Games

Cooperative Musical Circles

This game is a variation of Musical Chairs. Make three or four circles, including one circle that is larger than the others, on the floor with masking tape. Play a piece of music. Encourage the children to walk around the circles until the music stops. When the music stops, everyone steps into a circle. More than one child can stand in a circle. Remove a circle each time the music stops. Continue until there is only one circle left, the largest circle. The idea is to get everyone inside so everyone wins.

Duck, Duck, Goose

Children sit in a circle. One child, "IT", walks around the outside of the circle, tapping each player on the head and saying "Duck." Eventually IT taps a player and says "Goose" instead. The tapped player gets up and chases IT around the circle. If she taps IT before they get around the circle, she gets to go back to her place. If she doesn't, she becomes the new IT and the game continues.

Simon Says

Select a child to be Simon. Have Simon stand in front of the other children and give instructions. When Simon prefaces an instruction with "Simon Says" as in "Simon says stand up," the children stand up, and when Simon doesn't preface the instruction with "Simon Says" ("Stand up"), they

don't do it. For a fun, non-competitive version of this game, don't make children sit out for missing an instruction.

Tug of Peace

Take Hula Hoops® outdoors and encourage the children to play Tug of Peace. It takes cooperative effort. Have children sit around the Hula Hoop and grab hold with both hands. By pulling back on the hoop, can everyone stand up together?

School Days Facts

The Alphabet

- The English alphabet code lacks a one-to-one correspondence between sounds and symbols. Samuel Johnson standardized the spelling for words in 1755, but he did not standardize the spelling for sounds, or phonemes. As a result, there are multiple ways to spell most phonemes, and multiple ways to read most letters and digraphs, and these multiple ways don't match.
- All writing systems (alphabets), living or dead, are sound-based systems, not word-based.

Calendars

- Most of the oldest calendars were lunar calendars, based on the time interval from one new moon to the next, called a lunation.

Listening and Hearing

- Which activity involves the most amount of listening? Children spend 20 percent of all school-related hours just listening. If television viewing and half of conversations are included, children spend approximately 50 percent of their waking hours just listening. For those hours spent in the classroom, the amount of listening time can be almost 100 percent.

Music and Musical Instruments

○ Musical instruments are intended to produce sounds that are pleasing when heard in sequence, as in a melody, or at the same time, as in a chord. The pleasing pitches were long ago found to be described by small whole numbers, as in the lengths of the strings that produced them, or in their frequencies of vibration. These notes are called C, D, E, F, G, A, and B or do, re, mi, fa, sol, la, ti. This is called a diatonic scale with a keynote C. We are so used to this scale that we can sing it naturally, though it is a learned thing.

Nursery Rhymes

○ Humpty Dumpty was a powerful cannon during the English Civil War (1642-49). It was mounted on top of the St. Mary's at the Wall Church in Colchester to defend the city against siege in the summer of 1648. The church tower was hit by the enemy and the top of the tower was blown off, sending "Humpty" tumbling to the ground. Naturally the King's men tried to mend it but in vain.

○ The roots of the poem "Jack and Jill" are in France. Jack and Jill are said to be King Louis XVI (Jack) who was beheaded (lost his crown), followed by his Queen, Marie Antoinette (Jill) who "came tumbling after." The words and lyrics to the Jack and Jill poem were made more acceptable as a story for children by providing a happy ending!

Recipes

Bubble Solution #1

Mix 2 cups water with 1 cup dish soap (Dawn works great) and 1 cup glycerin. Let the mixture sit for at least 15 minutes, the longer the better.

Bubble Solution #2

Mix ⅔ cup Dawn™ dishwashing liquid and 1 tablespoon glycerin in one gallon of water. Let this solution sit for at least a day, preferably for a week.

Bubble Solution #3

Mix ¼ cup dishwashing detergent, ½ cup water, and 1 teaspoon sugar. Let stand for a few minutes.

No Tears Bubble Solution

Mix 12 cups water with 4 tablespoons glycerin. Add 1 cup Johnson's Baby Shampoo®.

Playdough #1

Combine 3 cups flour, 1½ cups salt, 3 tablespoons oil, 2 tablespoons cream of tartar, and 3 cups water. Cook over very low heat until mixture is no longer sticky to the touch. Store in an airtight container. This is nice, springy dough, close in texture to purchased playdough.

Playdough #2

Mix 6 cups flour, 3 cups salt, 2 cups water, ½ cup oil, and food coloring. Knead together. Store in an airtight container.

Celebration Cookies Rebus Recipe

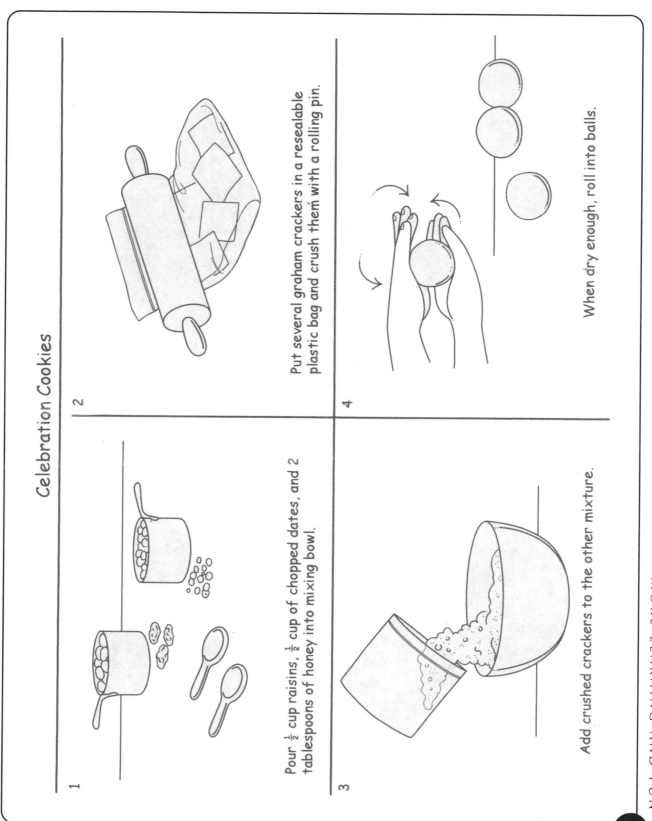

Celebration Cookies

1 Pour ½ cup raisins, ½ cup of chopped dates, and 2 tablespoons of honey into mixing bowl.

2 Put several graham crackers in a resealable plastic bag and crush them with a rolling pin.

3 Add crushed crackers to the other mixture.

4 When dry enough, roll into balls.

Cracker Stacker Rebus Recipe

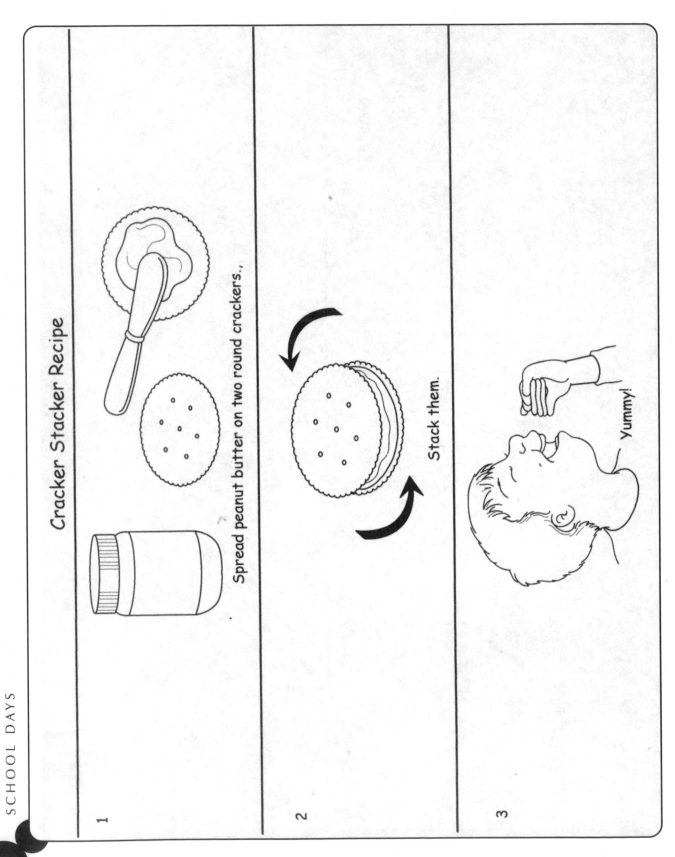

Cracker Stacker Recipe

1 Spread peanut butter on two round crackers.

2 Stack them.

3 Yummy!

Fruit Salad Rebus Recipe

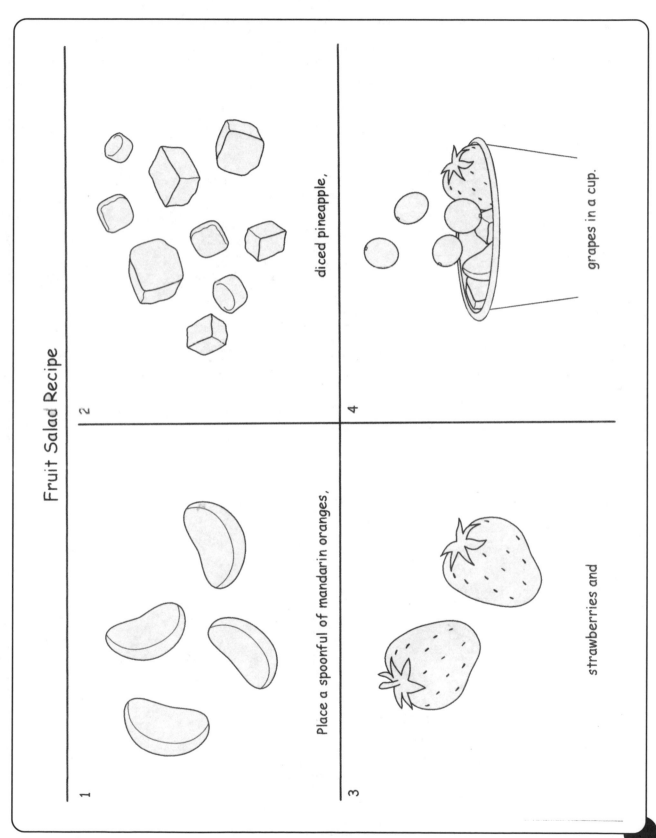

Fruit Salad Recipe

1

2 diced pineapple,

3 strawberries and

4 grapes in a cup.

Place a spoonful of mandarin oranges,

Green Drink Rebus Recipe

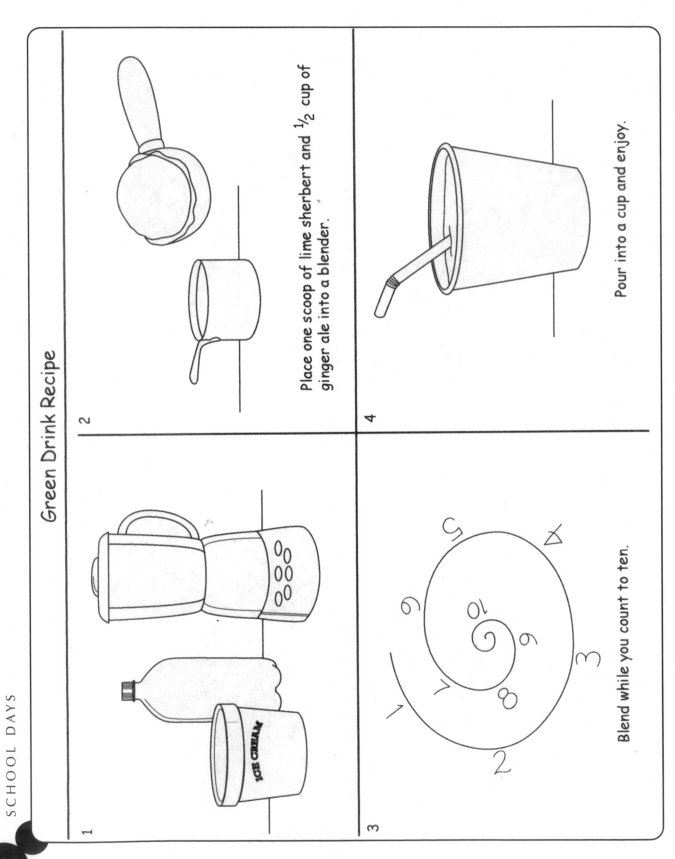

Green Drink Recipe

2 — Place one scoop of lime sherbert and 1/2 cup of ginger ale into a blender.

4 — Pour into a cup and enjoy.

1

3 — Blend while you count to ten.

Happy Face Pizza Rebus Recipe

Happy Face Pizza

100% Cheese

Mama's Pizza Sauce

Have the children brush on pizza sauce and then cover their muffin with pizza cheese.

Heat and eat!

Give each child one-half of an english muffin.

Provide olives and pepperoni sausages for the eyes and nose and slices of red bell peppers for the mouth.

Lemonade Rebus Recipe

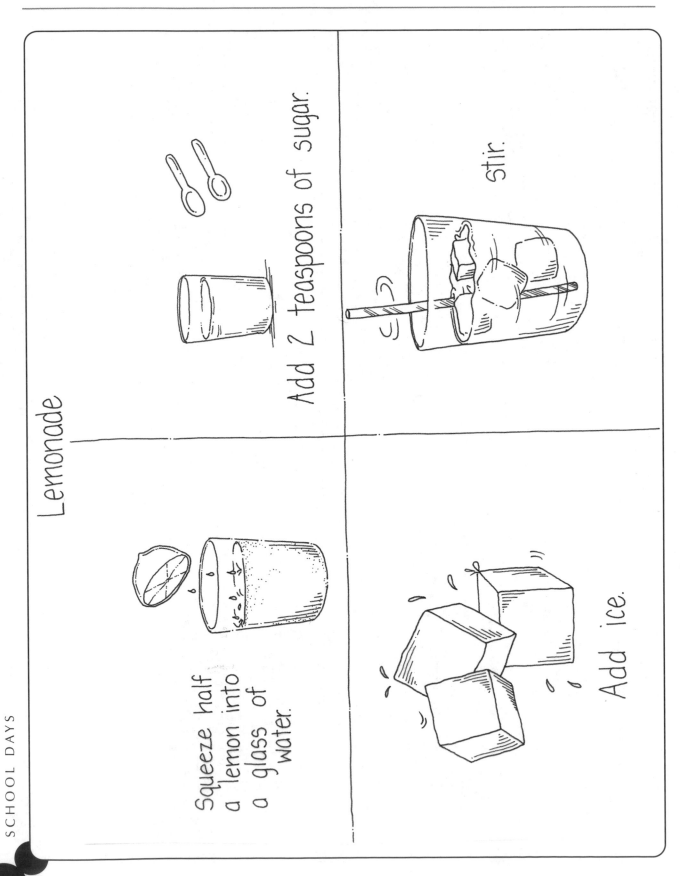

Lemonade

Squeeze half a lemon into a glass of water.

Add 2 teaspoons of sugar.

Add ice.

Stir.

Letter Pretzel Rebus Recipe

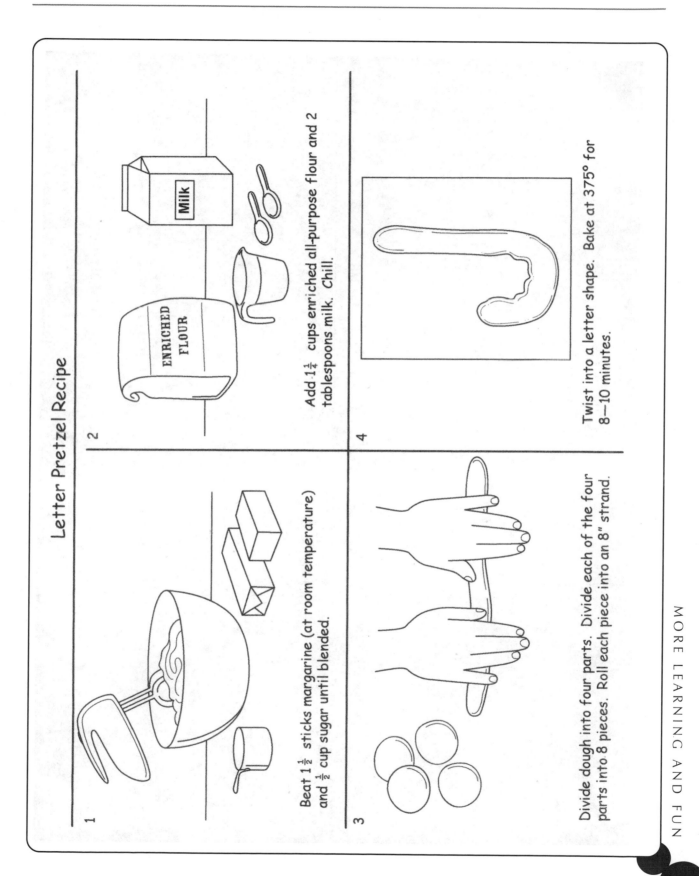

Letter Pretzel Recipe

1 Beat 1½ sticks margarine (at room temperature) and ½ cup sugar until blended.

2 Add 1¼ cups enriched all-purpose flour and 2 tablespoons milk. Chill.

3 Divide dough into four parts. Divide each of the four parts into 8 pieces. Roll each piece into an 8" strand.

4 Twist into a letter shape. Bake at 375° for 8–10 minutes.

Brushing My Teeth Sequence Cards

Color Rhyming Word Cards

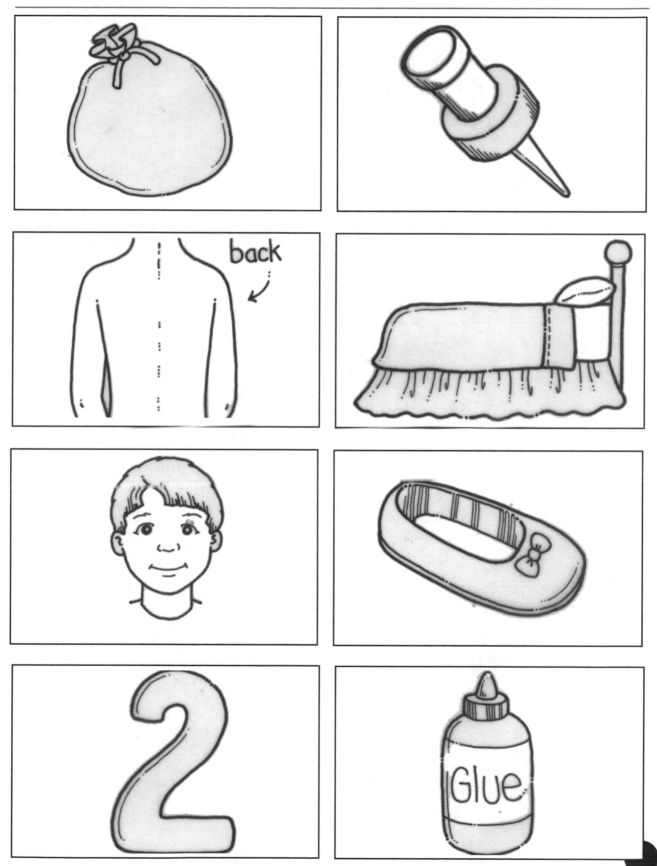

back

Glue

Day and Night Sorting Cards

Opposite Cards

Months of the Year Picture Cards

Months of the Year Picture Cards

July

August

September

October

November

December

Things That Go Together Cards

This Old Man Rhyming Word Cards

1

2

3

4

5

This Old Man Rhyming Word Cards

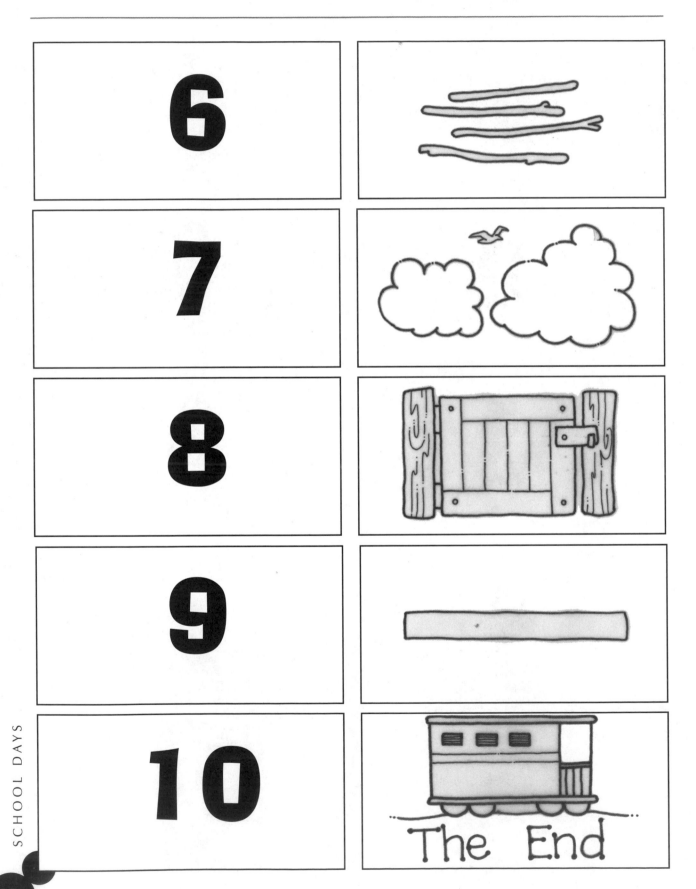

6

7

8

9

10

The End

American Sign Language Signs

feet

face

eye

ear

down

bubble

black

hello

head

happy birthday

happy

hand

green

fire

up

triangle

toy

stomach

school

nose

mouth

you

I love

References and Bibliography

Bulloch, K. 2003. *The mystery of modifying: Creative solutions.* Huntsville, TX: Education Service Center, Region VI.

Cavallaro, C. & M. Haney. 1999. *Preschool inclusion.* Baltimore, MD: Paul H. Brookes Publishing Company.

Gray, T. and S. Fleischman. Dec. 2004-Jan. 2005. "Research matters: Successful strategies for English language learners." *Educational Leadership,* 62, 84-85.

Hanniford, C. 1995. *Smart moves: Why learning is not all in your head.* Arlington, VA: Great Ocean Publications, p. 146.

Keller, M. 2004. "Warm weather boosts mood, broadens the mind." *Post Doctoral Study: The University of Michigan,* Anne Arbor, MI.

LeDoux, J. 1993. "Emotional memory systems in the brain." *Behavioral and Brain Research,* 58.

Theme Index

Animals, 16–18, 49–51

Clothing, 52–54

Colors, 37–39, 49–51, 75–78

Community workers, 46–48, 61–63, 70–71, 88–90

Counting, 16–18, 40–42, 70–71

Cultural diversity, 67–69

Day and night, 22–24

Family, 28–30, 43–45, 49–51, 79–81

Food, 37–39, 52–54, 75–78

Friends, 28–30, 43–45, 46–48, 52–54, 55–56, 82–84, 97–99

Health and safety, 88–90

Humor, 31–33

Make-believe, 49–51

Me, 25–27, 57–60, 82–84, 85–87, 94–96, 97–99

Music, 72–74

Numbers, 16–18, 70–71

Nursery rhymes, 64–66

Opposites, 19–21, 25–27, 64–66

Parts of the body, 57–60, 79–81

Seasons, 34–36

Senses, 57–60

Shapes and sizes, 40–42

Sounds, 16–18, 72–74, 85–87, 91–93

Spatial concepts, 64–66, 94–96

Toys, 43–45, 55–56

Under construction, 19–21

Children's Book Index

A

A My Name Is Alice by Jane Bayer, 87

Alexander, Who Used to Be Rich Last Sunday by Judith Viorst, 24

Alphabet Adventure by Audrey & Bruce Wood, 27

Alphabet Mystery by Audrey & Bruce Wood, 27

Animal Crackers: A Delectable Collection of Pictures, Poems, and Lullabies for the Very Young by Jane Dyer, 33

Animal Orchestra by Ilo Orleans, 69

Animal Orchestra by Scott Gustafson, 69

B

Baby Faces by Margaret Miller, 99

Beat the Drum! by Billy Davis, 74

Benny's Big Bubble by Jane O'Connor, 96

The Berenstain Bears and the Green-Eyed Monster by Stan & Jan Berenstain, 39

Black on White by Tana Hoban, 78

Brown Bear, Brown Bear, What Do You See? by Bill Martin Jr., 78

Bubble Bubble by Mercer Mayer, 87, 96

C

Caillou Puts Away His Toys by Joceline Sanschagrin, 56

Caps, Hats, Socks, and Mittens by Louise W. Borden, 54

The Cat in the Hat by Dr. Seuss, 56

Changes, Changes by Pat Hutchins, 71

Chicka Chicka Boom Boom by Bill Martin Jr. & John Archambault, 27

Chicken Soup and Rice: A Book of Months by Maurice Sendak, 36

Clifford Counts Bubbles by Norman Bridwell, 87

Color Farm by Lois Ehlert, 78

Colors by Chuck Murphy, 78

D

Down by the Bay by Raffi, 93

E

The Ear Book by Al Perkins, 60
Eating the Alphabet by Lois Ehlert, 27
Exactly the Opposite by Tana Hoban, 21

F

Fire Safety by Pati Myers Gross, 90
Fire! Fire! by Gail Gibbons, 90
"Fire! Fire!" Said Mrs. McGuire by Bill Martin Jr., 90
First Day Jitters by Julie Danneberg, 48
First Day, Hooray! by Nancy Poydar, 48, 63
Five Green and Speckled Frogs by Priscilla Burris, 39
From Head to Toe by Eric Carle, 81

G

Giggle Belly by Page Sakelaris, 99
Giggle, Giggle, Quack by Doreen Cronin, 99
Go Away, Big Green Monster! by Ed Emberley, 39
Good Morning, Good Night by Teresa Imperato, 30
Good Morning, Sam by Marie-Louise Gay, 30
Good Night, Sam by Marie-Louise Gay, 30
Goodnight Max by Rosemary Wells, 30
Goodnight Moon by Margaret Wise Brown, 30
The Grand Old Duke of York by Henry Sowden, 66
The Grand Old Duke of York by Maureen Roffey, 66
The Greedy Triangle by Marilyn Burns, 42
Green Eggs and Ham by Dr. Seuss, 39, 93

H

Head, Shoulders, Knees, and Toes by Annie Kubler, 81
Hearing by Maria Ruis, 60
Hello! Good-Bye! by Aliki, 30
Hurray for Pre-K by Ellen B. Senisi, 48, 84

L

Let's Count by Kelli Chipponeri, 71
The Listening Walk by Paul Showers, 60
Little Blue and Little Yellow by Leo Lionni, 87

M

Mary Wore a Red Dress and Henry Wore His Green Sneakers by Merle Peek, 51
Max Cleans Up by Rosemary Wells, 44
Meet the Orchestra by Ann Hayes, 74
Miss Bindergarten Gets Ready for Kindergarten by Joseph Slate, 48
Miss Mary Mack by Mary Ann Hoberman, 51
Musical Instruments From A to Z by Bobbie Kalman, 74
My First Spanish Word Book by DK Publications, 81
My Teacher's My Friend by P.K. Hallinan, 63

N

The Napping House by Audrey Wood, 30
Newton and the Big Mess by Rory Tyger, 44
No Dragons for Tea: Fire Safety for Kids by Jean Pendziwol, 90

O

One Fish, Two Fish, Red Fish, Blue Fish by Dr. Seuss, 93

One Windy Wednesday by Phyllis Root, 24
Our Marching Band by Lloyd Moss, 69, 74
Over, Under, Through, and Other Spatial Concepts by Tana Hoban, 96

P

Parade Day: Marching Through the Calendar by Bob Barner, 36
Perk Up Your Ears: Discover Your Sense of Hearing by Vicki Cobb, 60
Pigsty by Mark Teague, 44
Planting a Rainbow by Lois Ehlert, 78
Polar Bear, Polar Bear, What Do You Hear? by Bill Martin Jr., 60
Pop! A Book About Bubbles by Kimberly Brubaker Bradley, 96
The Principal's New Clothes by Stephanie Calmenson, 63

R

The Real Mother Goose Color Rhymes by Josie Yee, 33
The Real Mother Goose Sing-Along Rhymes by Josie Yee, 33
The Real Mother Goose by Blanche Fisher Wright, 33
Red, Blue, Yellow Shoe by Tana Hoban, 78

S

Shapes, Shapes, Shapes by Tana Hoban, 42
Sing a Song of Opposites by Pam Schiller, 21
Some Things Go Together by Charlotte Zolotow, 54
Song and Dance Man by Karen Ackerman, 69, 74
Stop, Drop, and Roll by Margery Cuyler, 90

T

Things That Go Together by Vincent Douglas, 54
This Little Train by Pam Schiller & Richele Bartkowiak, 78
This Old Man by Carol Jones, 18
This Old Man by Pam Adams, 18
This Old Man: A Pop-Up Song Book by Dick Dudley, 18
Today Is Monday by Eric Carle, 24
Toes Have Wiggles, Kids Have Giggles by Harriet Ziefert, 99
Toes, Ears, and Nose by Marion Dane Bauer, 81
Touch and Feel: Opposites: Garden by Ant Parker, 21
Triangles by Sarah L. Schuette, 42
Tub Toys by Terry Miller Shannon, 56
Tuesday by David Wiesner, 24
Twelve Hats for Lena: A Book of Months by Karen Katz, 36

V

The Very Hungry Caterpillar by Eric Carle, 24

W

Wacky Wednesday by Dr. Seuss, 24
Who Made This Big Mess? by Andrew Gutelle, 44
Will I Have a Friend? by Miriam Cohen, 63
Wordsong by Bill Martin Jr., 54

Z

Zin! Zin! Zin! Violin by Lloyd Moss, 69, 74

Index

A

Alliteration, 38, 50, 8
American Sign Language, 29, 34, 38, 40, 47, 49, 55, 65, 80, 83, 85, 88, 95, 98
    signs, 123–124
Art activities, 20, 29, 32, 38, 41, 47, 50, 53, 56, 68, 77, 80, 83, 86, 92, 95
Autism spectrum disorder, 21

B

Bags, 38, 48, 93, 107
Balls, 52, 81, 93
Beanbags, 19, 42, 59, 81, 89
Birthdays, 35–36
Blocks, 20, 32–33, 41, 44, 50, 53, 56, 65, 71, 83, 89, 93
    paper bag, 93
    triangular, 41
Boxes, 24, 50, 51, 54, 71, 73–74
Brain chemistry, 8
Bubbles, 85–87, 94–96
Buttons, 20, 24, 49, 50–51

C

Calendars, 23, 34, 36, 105
Cardboard tubes, 33, 54, 68, 73, 74
Cards
    Alphabet, 26
    Brushing My Teeth Sequence, 114
    Color Rhyming Words, 50, 77, 93, 115
    Day and Night Sorting, 116
    index, 63, 78, 84, 99
    Months of the Year Picture, 118–119
    Opposite, 21, 117
    Picture Months of the Year, 35
    Things That Go Together, 54, 120
    This Old Man Rhyming Word, 17–18, 121–123
Chants. *See* Rhymes
Cognitive challenges, 17, 53, 57, 39
Community workers, 46, 61, 70, 88
Compound words, 28
Comprehension activities, 8, 19, 28–29, 33, 40–41, 46, 52, 58, 76, 80, 83, 68, 71, 73, 80, 98
    special needs modifications, 76, 83
Cooking activities, 62, 89, 107–113
    English language learner strategies, 93
Counting activities, 18, 24, 51, 56
Craft sticks, 17, 24, 29, 78, 98

D

Dancing activities, 21, 48, 78, 84
Discovery activities, 20, 33, 65, 68, 73, 77, 86, 95
Dramatic play, 26, 33, 35, 38, 44, 47, 50, 53, 62, 65, 71, 83
Drums, 22, 54, 69, 73

E

English language learners
    involving in music, 11–12
    strategies for, 10 17, 20, 21, 34, 62–63, 78, 83, 89, 92–93
Environmental issues, 43–45

F

Fabric, 33, 46, 47, 59, 65
Field trips
    fire station, 89
    high school, 58, 68, 74
    park, 83
    school library, 63
    toy store, 56
Fine motor activities, 17, 21, 23, 26, 33, 38, 41, 44, 50, 53, 65, 71, 77, 81, 86, 89, 96, 99
Fingerplays
    April Clouds, 103
    Five Little Snowmen, 36, 103
    Where Is Thumbkin? 103
Fire safety, 88–90

G

Games
    Alphabet Hunt, 26
    Beanbag Catch, 41
    Cooperative Musical Chairs, 44, 105
    Don't Let the Ball Fall, 93
    Drop the Bag, 89
    Duck, Duck, Duke, 65
    Duck, Duck, Goose, 105
    English language learner strategies, 63
    Estómago, 81
    Gossip, 58
    Happy Face Concentration, 99
    Hopscotch, 24, 35
    Hula Hoops, 105, 38, 54, 96
    Loud and Soft Hide and Seek, 59
    The Principal Says, 63
    Red Light, Green Light, 39
    Simon Says, 59, 105
    Sock the Blocks, 93
    Stop and Go, 89
    Tug of Peace, 44
    Tummy Ticklers, 99
    Where's the Sound? 59
    Who Has the Button? 50
    You Can't Make Me Laugh, 99
Generalization skills, 76
Graphic organizers, 11–12
Graphing activities, 27, 36, 78
Gross motor activities, 18, 24, 33, 35, 42, 50, 63, 81, 89

H

Hearing impairments, 57
Home connections, 18, 21, 24, 30, 33, 36, 39, 42, 44, 48, 51, 54, 56, 60, 63, 66, 69, 71, 74, 78, 81, 84, 87, 90, 93, 96, 99
    English language learner strategies, 21

L

Laminate, 17–18, 21, 24, 33, 35, 50, 54, 66, 77, 93
Language development, 18, 21, 24, 26, 29–30, 35, 47, 50, 54, 63, 77, 93, 99
    special needs modifications, 21, 51
Learning
    expanding, 9
    optimizing, 8
Letter knowledge, 8, 26, 32, 41, 88, 91, 95
Library activities, 36, 48, 63
Listening skills, 7, 19, 26, 37, 57–60, 74, 84, 99, 105
    special needs modifications, 57, 73
Literacy concepts, 7–8, 16–17, 19–20, 23, 26, 28–29, 32, 34–35, 37–38, 40–41, 43–44, 46–47, 49–50, 52–53, 55, 58, 62, 65, 68, 70–73, 76, 80, 83, 85–86, 88–89, 91–92, 95, 98

M

Magnetic letters, 24, 26, 36, 42, 51, 93, 99
Markers, 18, 32, 41, 66, 74, 78, 92, 98
Masking tape, 18, 24, 33, 35, 42, 81, 89–90, 93, 105
Matching activities, 18, 51, 53–54
Math skills, 18, 24, 30, 36, 38, 42, 44, 48, 51, 59, 71, 74
    special needs modifications, 39
Measuring activities, 18, 21, 71
Memory skills, 97, 99
    optimizing, 8
Modeling, 11–12, 63
    by peers, 57, 95
Modifications
    special needs, 9, 17, 21–22, 39, 51. 53, 57, 61, 64, 73, 76, 87, 95, 98
Movement activities, 21, 18, 27, 48, 56, 60, 66, 69, 74, 78, 84, 93
    special needs modifications, 69
Music, 106
    activities, 18, 21, 24, 30, 36, 48, 51, 54, 56, 60, 66, 69, 74, 78, 81, 84, 93, 96
    expanding learning, 9
    in the early years, 7
    marching, 69
    special needs modifications, 69
Musical instruments, 72–73, 106
    rhythm band, 18, 58–59, 69, 72–74

O

Onomatopoeia, 8, 68, 98
Oral language development, 7, 16, 20, 23, 29, 34, 38, 41, 43–44, 47, 49, 52–53, 55, 58, 62, 65, 68, 70, 76, 80, 83, 85–86, 88–89, 95, 98
    English language learner strategies, 20, 34, 62, 89
    special needs modifications, 53, 98
Outdoor activities, 39, 44, 56, 66, 78, 87, 96
    special needs modifications, 87

P

Paint, tempera, 17, 20, 38, 47, 68, 83, 86, 95
Paintbrushes, 20, 38, 50, 53, 68
Paper, 17, 20, 32, 38, 41, 44, 47, 50, 52, 58, 63, 68, 74, 80, 83–84, 86, 92, 95, 99
    butcher, 87
    chart, 18, 23–24, 26, 28, 32, 35, 38, 41, 42, 47–48, 62–63, 69, 71, 73–74, 83, 86, 88, 90–91, 95, 98–99
    construction, 29, 33, 38, 42, 66, 77, 80, 93
    crepe, 78
    drawing, 32, 48, 51, 83, 90
    easel, 41
    newspaper, 24, 33, 65, 93
    thick, 39
    tracing, 78
    wax, 68
Paper bags, 44, 93
Paper plates, 29, 78, 98
Patterning activities, 17, 38, 42, 52–53, 74, 92
Peer modeling, 57, 95
Pencils, 47, 52, 58–59, 63, 73–74
Phonological awareness, 8, 17, 26, 32, 38, 50, 53, 68, 76, 86, 91–92, 98
    English language learner strategies, 17, 92
Photocopiers, 17–18, 21, 23, 35, 50, 54, 77, 93
Pictures, 11
    animals, 39
    happy faces, 99
    musical instruments, 68, 73
Plastic
    animals, 32
    bags, 38, 107
    eggs, 33, 66
    food, 48, 62
    knives, 54, 108
    people, 65
    tubing, 77, 86, 95
Playdough, 17, 21, 26, 41, 65, 77, 83, 99
Pocket charts, 20
Poems. *See* Rhymes
Popsicle sticks. *See* Craft sticks
Print awareness, 8, 17, 20, 23, 35, 38, 47, 55, 62, 71, 73, 76, 80, 83, 98
    English language learner strategies, 62
    special needs modifications, 17
Puppets, 29, 33, 80, 83, 98
Puzzles, 24, 33, 52–53, 66, 83

R

Rebus drawings, 84
Recipes
    bubble solution, 106
    celebration cookies, 62, 89, 107
    cracker stackers, 93, 108
    fruit salad, 78, 109
    green drink, 39, 110
    green goop, 38
    happy face pizza, 99, 111
    lemonade, 78, 112
    letter pretzels, 27, 113
    playdough, 106
    rebus, 27, 39, 62, 67, 89, 93, 99, 107–113

Recorded music, 21, 56, 66, 69, 74, 78, 84, 93, 105
Rhymes
    Big and Small, 20
    Good Morning, 102
    Good Night and Good Morning, 102
    Hey Diddle Diddle, 32
    In the Merry Month of May, 102
    Little Boy Blue, 32
    Monday's Child, 23
    Say and Touch, 92
    Thirty Days, 35
Rhyming activities, 8, 17, 26, 32, 50, 53, 76–77, 86, 91–93
Rhythm band instruments, 18, 58–59, 69, 72–74

S

Science activities, 39, 60, 63, 66, 87, 96
Segmentation activities, 8, 17, 23, 58
Sentence strips, 20, 24
Sequencing activities, 26, 35, 58
Snacks
    bubbly drinks, 87, 96
    celebration cookies, 62
    cracker stackers, 93
    curds and whey, 33
    fruit salad, 78
    green drink, 39
    happy face pizza, 99
    lemonade, 78
    letter pretzels, 27
    opposite, 60
    opposites, 21
    peanut butter and jelly sandwiches, 44, 54
    quiet and noisy, 21, 60
Social studies, 44, 69
Songs
    The Alphabet Song, 25–27
    April Clouds, 36
    Are You Listening? 57–60
    B-B-B-Bubbles, 85–87, 94
    The Bubble Song, 96, 100
    Bubbles in the Air, 85, 94–96
    The Bubbles Soar Over the Playground, 96, 100
    Can You Put the Toys Away? 43, 45, 55–56
    Clap, Tap, Snap, 92
    Clean Up, 43–45, 54, 56
    The Color Song, 75–78
    Dance of the Toy Soldiers from *The Nutcracker*, 56
    Days of the Week, 22–24
    Do You Know the Principal? 61–63
    Good Morning to You, 28–30, 100
    Good Morning, 100
    The Grand Old Duke of York, 64–66
    Great Green Gobs, 37–39
    Happy Birthday, 34
    Happy Faces, 97–99
    The Hokey Pokey, 60
    I Like School, 82–84
    In the Merry, Merry Month of May, 36, 101
    Itsy Bitsy Spider, 81
    Jingle Bells, 81
    Johnny Works With One Hammer, 70–71
    Lazy Mary, Will You Get Up? 51, 101

    Little Miss Muffet, 32
    MacNamara's Band, 67–69
    Mary Had a Little Lamb, 51, 101
    Mary, Mary, Quite Contrary, 51, 101
    Miss Mary Mack, 36, 49–51, 101
    Months of the Year, 34–36
    The Mulberry Bush, 24, 100–101
    My Hands on My Head, 79–81, 99, 101–102
    Nursery Rhyme Rap, 31–33
    Old MacDonald Had a Band, 72–74
    Peanut Butter and Jelly, 52
    Remember, Remember, 32
    Rhyme Time, 91–93
    Ring Around the Rosie, 32
    School Days, 46–48
    Sing a Song of Opposites, 19–21
    Stop, Drop, and Roll, 88–90
    This Is the Way We Brush Our Teeth, 102
    This Old Man, 16–18
    Three Straight Sides, 40–42
    What Goes Together? 52–54
Sorting activities, 21, 26, 42, 44, 51, 56, 76
Spatial concepts, 64, 94
Special needs children
    modifications for, 9, 17, 21–22, 39, 51. 53, 57, 61, 64,
        73, 76, 87, 95, 98
Stories
    I Like School, 46, 83, 104
    Mrs. Wiggle and Mrs. Waggle, 19, 103–104
    Sammy the Seahorse, 58, 104–105
Story maps, 11
Story time, 21, 24, 63
Strategies, for English language learners, 10 17, 20, 21, 34,
    62–63, 78, 83, 89, 92–93
Synonyms, 12

T

Tape recorders, 59, 74, 84, 99
Tape, masking, 18, 24, 33, 35, 42, 81, 89–90, 93, 105
Tempera paint, 17, 20, 38, 47, 68, 83, 86, 95
Toilet paper tubes, 33, 68, 74
Tolerance, 57
Tongue depressors. *See* Craft sticks
Triangle templates, 41

V

Visual aids, 11
Visual challenges, 39
Vocabulary, 16, 19, 22, 25, 28, 31, 34, 37, 40, 43, 46, 49, 52,
    57, 61, 64, 67, 70–72, 75, 79, 82, 85, 88, 91, 94, 97

W

Wallpaper samples, 47, 77
Water play, 21, 44
Word webs, 11
Writing activities, 18, 24, 30, 36, 42, 48, 51, 56, 63, 69, 74,
    78, 84, 90, 99